The Food Almanac

RECIPES AND STORIES FOR A YEAR AT THE TABLE

By Miranda York

ILLUSTRATIONS BY LOUISE SHEERAN

PAVILION

Contents

Good Things

'Anyone who likes to eat, can soon learn to cook well,' begins Jane Grigson's
Good Things, a stylish collection of cookery articles and recipes from one of the
great pioneers of 20th-century food writing. I've always believed this: that a
fascination with food, with how to make it delicious and how to get the most
pleasure from it, is all that's needed to cook and eat well. It's easy to get distracted
by flashy new techniques or the latest superfood, but, as the chef and restaurateur
Fergus Henderson observes: 'Trends are a tragedy in food – they condemn the
sublime to the realm of the temporary, or they elevate the flimsy beyond its merit.
Good things should be a constant and cooked with conviction.'

And so, to put it very simply, this is a book about good things to eat. It's also a
collection of brilliant writing by some of the most talented cooks and scribes,
from legendary food writers and lauded chefs to up-and-coming poets and debut
novelists. You'll find memoirs, essays, short stories and poems alongside recipes,
menus and monthly reading lists, presented within the framework of a seasonal
food almanac: a month-by-month guide to the culinary year. Each chapter begins

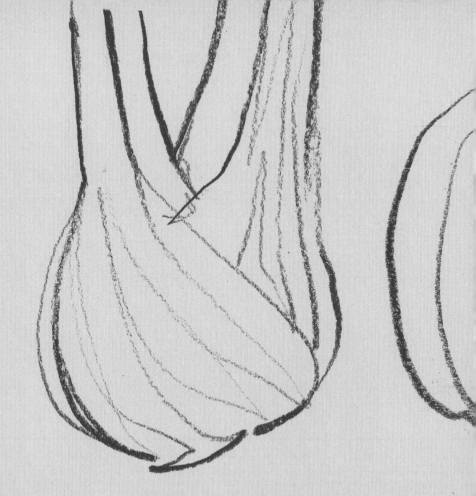

with an introduction to the month ahead, followed by seasonal highlights for the larder, spotlights on ingredients and passages on food history. The chapters end with a menu, each recipe carefully chosen to show off the best of the season, and a reading list, should you wish to delve deeper into the ingredients explored and the stories told.

As you may have guessed, this is not a traditional almanac. It won't tell you about the tides and the phases of the moon, list the times for sunrise and sunset, or suggest when to sow seeds and harvest crops. It will tell you the best time to eat each harvest, though, and I hope the following pages will spark ideas and intrigue and inspire, weaving practical advice and recipes through stories that are at once universal and intensely personal. This is not a manual, dictating and reprimanding, but a book about enjoying food. It's about cooking in harmony with the seasons: how it can be a pleasure, not a chore, to follow the rhythms of the growing year. There's a sense of anticipation as the landscape changes around us, and there's joy to be found in the bounty it brings.

As well as looking to contemporary writers for their thoughts on food, I've borrowed from the great cookery writers of the past, in particular Jane Grigson, M.F.K. Fisher, Elizabeth David and Margaret Costa, their wise and witty words a constant companion as I write. I admire their attitude to cooking and eating, their appetite for both food and knowledge. They have written books to live with and learn from, books to keep among the pots and pans, or scatter across the kitchen table, well-thumbed and reassuringly familiar. 'No one who cooks cooks alone,' said the American novelist Laurie Colwin. 'Even at her most solitary, a cook in the kitchen is surrounded by generations of cooks past.' I look to these writers for guidance, and perhaps also because of a niggling feeling that we've lost something of our food culture over the years – our connection to the land and the seasons, and to our culinary heritage. To reclaim it, we must look to the past and the future. This is not nostalgia, but a practical way to fill in the blanks – though there's always room for a little romance in the kitchen, too.

Although this book is rooted in the British seasons, there's an openness to the influences of the constantly shifting world around us. 'No cookery belongs exclusively to its country, or its region,' said Jane Grigson. 'Cooks borrow – and always have borrowed – and adapt through the centuries.' It's therefore difficult to be purist about British cookery, or any country's cooking for that matter. And as individuals, we each draw on our own experiences and history to form our personal repertoire. So yes, you'll find notes and stories on whisky, wild garlic, apples and quinces, the joy of toast and the comfort of puddings, picnics and English seaside snacks, but also pieces about Malaysian durian, Caribbean Carnival, Chinese New Year, Australian Anzac biscuits, Nigerian efo riro, Venetian cichèti, Canadian maple syrup, Middle Eastern ma'amoul and Californian Meyer lemons.

I hope this volume will be both a companion in the kitchen and a book to curl up with; that you'll enjoy the literary musings on food, cook recipes from the carefully curated menus and perhaps learn something new along the way. Food can be a portal to other worlds and a tool to illuminate broader subjects; it can embody the anthropology of a culture. But I'll refrain from grandiose statements and look once more to my favourite food writers. Diana Henry simplifies it wonderfully: 'Cooking and eating is about taking pleasure in the things that are quite ordinary in a way.' And in the end, it's about appetite. As M.F.K. Fisher once said, 'First we eat. Then we do everything else.'

MIRANDA YORK

A Note on Seasonality

The seasons cannot be rigidly defined; they are unpredictable and ever-changing. Apply a similar attitude to the way you use and interpret this book, flicking to the chapters either side of your chosen month for recipes and culinary inspiration.

In each chapter you'll find a 'cook's larder' on the opening page, followed by a spotlight on a seasonal ingredient. These lists draw attention to some of the highlights of the season, a quick reference to provide instant ideas when you're shopping for your supper. The lists lean towards British produce, although there are specialities from our neighbours, too. With the exception of forced produce (such as rhubarb, radicchio and sea kale), the lists refer to fruit and vegetables that mature outdoors without artificial heat or shelter. You'll also discover wild foods to forage from the fields, woods and hedgerows, followed by game whose quality or availability varies significantly with the seasons. Finally, a small and highly subjective selection of cheeses, which are surprisingly seasonal despite their year-round availability (flick to May and December to find out why). The recommendations come from two excellent cheese shops: Paxton & Whitfield and La Fromagerie.

Most fruit and vegetables are now available all year round, whether it's because we've found clever ways of extending the seasons or because produce is shipped to us from the other side of the world. The edges have blurred and the idea of seasonality has been all but forgotten. Yet there's still something special about dipping spears of crisp asparagus into soft yolks in spring, biting into the perfect peach in summer, gently moving wild mushrooms around a pan frothing with salted butter in autumn, and peeling a jewel-like blood orange, its citrus mist thrilling the senses, on a grey winter's day. Eating with the seasons brings a rich variety to our lives and is, of course, more sustainable. But most satisfying of all, it tastes better. Flavour should always win.

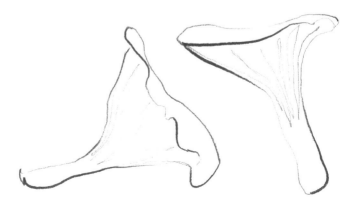

January

THE COOK'S LARDER

Ingredients to look out for in January:

- Blood oranges, lemons, Seville oranges
- January King cabbage, Jerusalem artichokes, kale, radicchio
- Black mustard leaves
- Hare, venison
- Gruyère, Lanark Blue

Beginning the year in the depths of winter can feel overbearing, but, viewed in a different light, the prolonged darkness becomes cosseting, offering a chance for repose. 'Nothing can be as peaceful and endless as a long winter darkness', wrote the Finnish author Tove Jansson – and Finns, of all people, know what it is to experience the extremes of this season.

January is a time to recentre, restock, move slowly. Is there a better excuse to spend time in the kitchen, enveloped by steam and bathed in the warm glow of the oven, than a grey day that neither tempts nor necessitates being outdoors? Bright citrus fruits come into season just when we need them most, and making preserves will lengthen their influence: bitter Seville oranges made into marmalade; perhaps lemons too, although a classic lemon curd cannot be beaten.

It isn't just fruit that peacocks in the greengrocer's window. January King cabbages can survive the winter chill, their blue-green leaves splashed with burgundy, the colour intensifying with each frost. Bitter leaves come into their own – blousy pink radicchios, endive spears tipped with gold, and the palest Castelfranco flecked with claret – cleansing the palate and prettying our plates thanks to the dark art of forcing.

Dabble in resolutions if you will, but most important of all, begin the year as you should begin every day, with a good breakfast. Elizabeth David said, 'One of the main points about the enjoyment of food and wine seems... to lie in having what you want *when* you want it and in the particular combination you fancy.' So eat cake for breakfast (you'll find a recipe at the end of the chapter) or breakfast for dinner – all under the cover of darkness.

Lemons

Citrus fruits bring flashes of brightness to the dull grey days of January. For the cook, they are welcome saviours, arriving just in time to lift the flavours of dwindling winter produce. Unlike Seville and blood oranges, whose arrival we eagerly await, we rarely think of lemons as a seasonal fruit. After all, they're available all year round. Yet Italian lemons, such as Amalfi and Sorrento, are worth seeking out in winter; their irregular beauty contains an intensely fragrant juice, the skins are softer, the pith less bitter.

It's easy to toss a few lemons into a shopping basket without a second thought, so common is the sight of their vibrant yellow skin, but in the 16th century, when vinegar and verjuice (the juice of unripe grapes) were used to add acid piquancy to dishes, lemons were the ultimate luxury. At a banquet for Henry VIII and Anne Boleyn in 1533, it is recorded that 'among the princely luxuries which graced the feast was one lemon'. Just one.

Today, it's hard to imagine cooking without lemons. Perhaps more than any other ingredient, this elliptical fruit has the power to transform a dish. It has the rare ability to both distinguish and harmonise: drawing more clearly into view each ingredient, while uniting disparate flavours. Lemon juice enhances savoury qualities, brings out the sweetness of other fruits, prevents discolouration and tenderises or 'cooks' food without heat. Lemons are vital to everyday cooking. 'There are indeed times,' said Elizabeth David, 'when a lemon as a seasoning seems second only in importance to salt.'

WHAT TO DO WITH LEMONS

- Dry the zest and add to jars of sugar or salt.
- Make a light syrup with the peel for poaching fruit.
- Beat the zest into ricotta and add to soups or broths.
- Eat the whole fruit: try deep-fried slices (a signature fritto item at Zuni Café in San Francisco) or make lemon sandwiches – thin slices of soft-skinned lemons between thickly buttered wholemeal bread – to serve with smoked salmon.
- Pack the fruit into large jars with salt for a few months to make preserved lemons, or cheat by simmering the pared zest for an instant version (look to Anna Hansen's *The Modern Pantry* for the recipe).
- Infuse honey with the zest, and play with flavour combinations by adding herbs and spices.

Meyer Lemons

THE ADVENTURES OF A DAREDEVIL BOTANIST

The plump, orange-tinted Meyer lemon is sweeter and juicier than other lemons, with a heady perfume that sends chefs and home cooks into rapture. Most lemons deliver a lightning bolt of acidity, but Meyers have a mellow sweetness when picked at their peak, bathed in California's golden winter sunshine.

For a fruit so cherished by gardeners and coveted by chefs, the Meyer lemon has a dramatic past with more plot twists than a best-selling mystery. It was discovered in China in 1907 by the botanical explorer Frank Nicholas Meyer, whose adventures would sound too outlandish to be credible had he not documented them in great detail: he was regularly threatened and robbed on his travels, attacked by bears, tigers and wolves, and accused of being the devil by people who had never before seen a white man.

Yet Frank Meyer persevered. He trekked across China and gathered thousands of new plant varieties – from soybeans and oats to persimmons, wild pears and asparagus – to bring back to America. He promised his family, 'I will be famous. Just wait a century or two,' before dying in mysterious circumstances after falling from a steamboat bound for Shanghai.

Despite Meyer's untimely end, the lemons he discovered flourished in California, ripening in the Central Valley from November until March, and even year-round along parts of the coast. The Meyer lemon is now emblematic of the local foodways and, like so many facets of Californian cuisine, its recent popularity can arguably be traced to Berkeley's famed Chez Panisse, where founder Alice Waters and pastry chef Lindsey Shere showcased the fruit in many of their recipes. In the early days, the lemons were foraged from parks and backyards, then sliced, squeezed and zested into lemon meringue pies, ice creams, sorbets and soufflés.

When Chez Panisse opened on April Fool's Day in 1980, Alice Waters wrote that she wanted 'to create a community of friends, lovers, and relatives that spans generations and is in tune with the seasons, the land, and human appetites'. At the time this was a radical notion, and it has influenced the food world more than we perhaps realise. One restaurant changed the way we eat, just as one piece of fruit, plucked from a small tree found beside a family's doorway in China a century ago, changed the landscape and cooking of a faraway land.

Lemons at My Table
by Deborah Levy

It has often occurred to me that the eggs and lemons in my kitchen are the most beautiful things in my home. I see no reason to hide either in the fridge and instead place them centre stage in a bowl on my dining table. They are sculptures, each of them a one-off, despite their similarity in form and colour. Eggs have the added uncanny allure of being an artwork that is made inside the body of a hen. Freud, who disliked eating chicken, apparently once shouted, 'Let the chickens live and lay eggs'. I agree, although I admit that I don't always listen to Freud and sometimes roast a chicken, usually with a lemon stuffed inside.

It's uplifting to glance at a bowl of sunny lemons with their startling palette of yellows on a cold British winter morning. I have been lucky enough in my life to have spent summers walking down a mountain to a beach in Majorca through lemon orchards that eventually lead to the sea. By the end of summer, many of the lemons have fallen to the ground and lie scattered below the trees. I often think about this walk when I buy a lemon from my local London corner shop in January. Shivering in the rain, I know that the lemon (and I) would rather be in that orchard, and that we are both migrants.

When I first came to England from Africa, aged nine, my new best friend brought lemon curd sandwiches to school. I had never heard of such an exotic thing as lemon curd. The bread was white and soft with a thin stripe of the sweet yellow paste just visible between the slices. My friend came from a religious Christian family and always said grace before she ate her packed lunch. For a while, I associated lemon curd with a higher spiritual force, as if it were a substance somehow entwined with God. When she shared her sandwiches with me, I thought they were holy.

Years later, I remembered my childhood friend when I was living in Paris and tasted every lemon curd pastry at my local boulangerie. Sometimes the curd was flavoured with thyme or lavender, but it is still a *parfait* tarte au citron, eaten slowly while sipping a small espresso, that represents my enduring romance with Europe. So, too, does the pasta sauce I make with lemon juice, Parmesan and olive oil. I feel sophisticated when I eat this dish, but slightly sick as well. Oddly, this has never put me off making it.

At Christmas my daughters pierce lemons with cloves and we decorate the table with them for the feast. In their teenage years, they would squeeze lemon juice on their hair, believing it would 'bring out the highlights'. I'm not sure it did, but the juice was youthful, like them. They were excited to think their hair might develop new, unknown dimensions.

The taste and fragrance of lemon rind has a totally different mood from its juice: the oil in the skin, particularly when used as a 'twist' for a dry vodka martini, is intense, deep, flamboyant, serene, while the juice is perhaps slightly neurotic. Yet when the juice, along with finely grated lemon zest and sea salt, is added to Greek yogurt, it metamorphoses into something otherworldly. Guided by the great Yotam Ottolenghi, I add roasted tomatoes that have caramelised with olive oil and cumin to the cold lemon yogurt. Really, I see no reason to ever eat anything else again.

I am staring at the bowl of unwaxed lemons on my table right now. Wax is used to preserve the freshness of their skin and protect them in transit, but as I mostly use their zest, these are the lemons of my choice. Given the beauty of their form, I am not surprised they have been muses and models for many famous artists. Sometimes a lemon has had to take off its peel when posing for a still life, but it is more usual to see it resting on a plate, happy in its own skin.

A Toast to Whisky

by Signe Johansen

Winter-evening cold.
Our backs might never warm up but our faces
Burned from the hearth-blaze and the hot whiskeys.
Seamus Heaney

Midwinter amber skies at sunset and sunrise are Mother Nature's reminder to us to seek comfort and joy where we can find it; so take a moment and pour yourself a glass of 'liquid sunshine', as George Bernard Shaw described this most soothing of spirits.

While the history of beer and wine stretches back thousands of years, alcoholic spirits arrived in Europe more recently, around the 8th century, thanks to contact with Arab chemists who pioneered the technique of distillation for medicinal purposes. *Uisge-beatha* and *usquebaugh* – both Gaelic words for whisky – are translations of the Latin *aqua vitae*, or 'water of life', a clue to the supposed restorative qualities of these potent spirits.

The earliest written record of whisky is from the 15th century and for much of its early history the spirit was associated with enterprising monks in Scotland and Ireland. Emigrants from those countries brought a taste for whisky and, crucially, the knowledge of how to make it to the American colonies, where Founding Father and US President James Madison famously consumed a pint of the stuff every day.

Good quality whisky is still associated with Scotland, malt whisky in particular, thanks to the successful branding of Scottish distilleries and blends. Scotland has five whisky-producing regions: Speyside, Highland, Lowland, Islay and Campbeltown. As writer Rachel McCormack notes in her whisky travelogue *Chasing the Dram: Finding the Spirit of Whisky*, the flavours are lighter in the Lowlands and those big peaty drams are usually to be found on Islay. Head east to west in the Highlands and you'll discover that the local whiskies are both smoky and peaty. There are exceptions in each region, so be wary of cleaving too fiercely to those descriptors.

On 25 January each year Scotland celebrates its national bard, Robert Burns. In recent years, the Burns Night tradition of feasting on haggis (a delicious savoury pudding made from offal, oats, onions and spices) and toasting the poet with whisky has become increasingly popular beyond Scottish borders. 'O thou, my muse! guid auld Scotch drink!' proclaimed Burns in his poem 'Scotch Drink'.

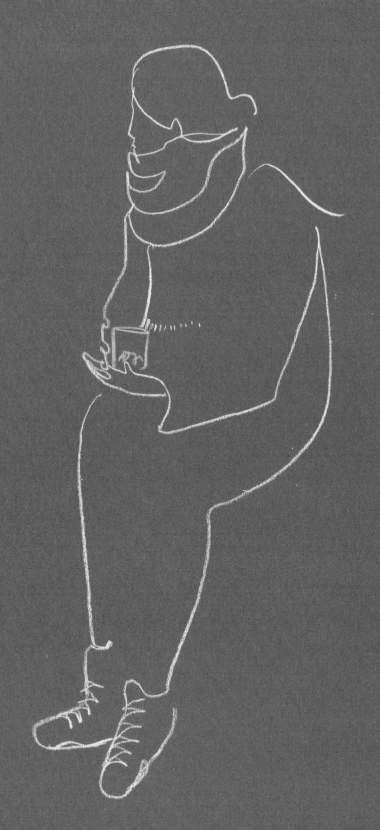

But when the sea is a shade of weathered pewter, Christmas trees have been unceremoniously dumped and the January blues threaten to descend, why wait until the 25th for that celebratory dram? Grab a book of poems, head outdoors, embrace the cold and take a small flask of whisky to sip when you stop for a reading break. Make *drambling* your New Year's pursuit.

Slàinte mhath, as they say in Scotland. To your good health.

WAYS TO ENJOY WHISKY

- Islay Scotch such as Lagavulin matches perfectly with Maltesers. Next time you're braving the January squalls and out on a coastal dramble, try it.

- Peaty whisky matches surprisingly well with blue cheese.

- A classic sponge cake iced with a simple whisky glaze makes a welcome change from butter icings.

- Make a mild hot toddy by mixing apple juice, whole spices (clove, cinnamon, star anise, green cardamom, black pepper), sliced fresh ginger, a peel of lemon and a tot of whisky. Decant into a Thermos and take it with you to recharge after your next cold-water swim.

- As a nod to the Auld Alliance between Scotland and France, soak a handful of Agen prunes in whisky. Steep overnight or until the prunes become plump, then decant a few into a small bowl. Add a spoonful of whipped cream or crème fraîche, drizzle over some of the whisky and crumble a shortbread over the top.

- If you have some prunes left over, leave them to marinate in a large glass jar for a few weeks, removing one when you feel the urge for a strong coffee – the combination is remarkably revivifying.

SCOTCH RIVALS

In Ireland and the USA an 'e' is added, hence *whiskey*, whereas Scotch is *whisky*. There is no definitive answer as to why this is the case, except that the Irish are thought to have added an 'e' simply to differentiate their spirit from their Scottish rivals.

January Has Been Waiting for You

by Selina Nwulu

January arrives after the gluttony of December,
moving as languidly as the sunrise in the mornings.
A whole new month to remember yourself,
to recentre for the days ahead.
Restock the tea selection, fall in love
with a new recipe. Start a new hobby
that maybe you'll stick with, or maybe you won't.
Make plans while the calendar is still empty
enough for dreaming. Open the pantry
to a jumble of vegetables who knew you'd return,
however sheepishly. Give brussels sprouts
their chance to shine without the fame of turkey,
take a bite of radicchio, its bittersweet hand
a blossoming invitation. Turn the gnarled knuckle
of celeriac into a mash with a generous knob of butter
and sprinkle of pepper. Take yourself out for an afternoon
walk, just before the sun begins to set, listen
to your feet crunch the ice on the ground, keep going
until the tip of your nose is numb. Welcome yourself back
with a hearty vegetable stew and dumplings, a tart
rhubarb crumble eaten by the comfort of a lavish fire.
January has been waiting for you to work up
an appetite, savour it.

A Menu for January

by Ella Risbridger

Pikelets are like crumpets, but untidy. Pikelets shouldn't be perfect or precise. In fact, with pikelets, every imperfection is proof that you did it all by yourself. I love recipes like this. There's something brilliant about a recipe that doesn't ask too much of you; a recipe, in fact, where getting it exactly right would be exactly wrong; a recipe you can fiddle with, and tend to when you remember. The bicarb here gives both a slight sour tang, and a gentle rise; it's not in all pikelet recipes, but I really like it. If you're on your own, I suggest you make the full quantity anyway. The cooked pikelets will be fine in an airtight container for a few days, and you can toast them in a regular toaster without hassle. I confess I have never been able to keep pikelets in the house without eating them for longer than about four days, so I don't know how well they keep past that point.

Serves 4

175g (6oz) plain (all-purpose) flour
1 x 7g (¼oz) sachet instant yeast
½ tsp caster (superfine) sugar
½ tsp fine salt
½ tsp bicarbonate of soda (baking soda)
150ml (5fl oz) milk
150ml (5fl oz) hot water
Oil, for frying, if your frying pan (skillet) isn't non-stick
Butter and jam, Marmite or strong Cheddar, to serve

So. Breakfast. You get up, and put the kettle on for tea. While the kettle's boiling, you measure everything out: dry ingredients into a big bowl, and milk into a jug. When the kettle boils, pour the hot water into the jug with the milk (and the rest into the teapot). Stir to a sort of baby's bath temperature, so it feels pleasant on the back of your hand, neither too cold nor too hot – and when it gets there (no hotter, please), pour it into the bowl with the dry ingredients.

Now whisk like billy-o. Keep whisking: 3–4 minutes of whisking with your whole strength. Come on, you'll get an hour to rest in a minute… This puts the

holes in the pikelet, which sounds like an old-fashioned idiom for breaking something ('By Jove, that's put the holes in the pikelet!') but isn't: the bubbles of air you're beating into the mixture become the holes when you griddle it.

Cover the bowl with a clean tea towel, and take your tea back to bed.

After an hour or so (it'll stand a little bit longer, so don't worry if you're at a good bit of your book, or otherwise occupied), come back and check the mixture. It should be bubbly and frothy and about half as big again as when you left it. Stick your largest frying pan over a medium heat, adding a drizzle of oil if your pan's not non-stick. Get someone else to put butter and jam on the table, or butter and Marmite, or thin potato-peeler strips of cheese.

Take a tablespoonful of your batter and dollop it into the hot pan. Repeat a couple more times, depending on the size of your pan; leave some space in between for the pikelets to spread out. Cook for about 90 seconds, then flip over with a spatula and give them another 60 seconds.

Use the spatula to lift your pikelets out onto a plate. Drape immediately with cheese, or a hunk of best butter as thick as a thumb.

by Yotam Ottolenghi

January is the best time to eat veg that has been hiding away under the surface over winter, protecting itself from the elements. Celeriac is one of my favourites, not least because it's so versatile: grated raw in a salad, as you would beetroot or carrot; mashed as an alternative to potato; roasted whole or in a gratin; blitzed in a soup. This dish can be eaten at any time of the day as a light meal or starter, but it's particularly good for brunch, perhaps with some crisp bacon.

Makes 10 rösti, to serve 2 to 4

1 celeriac, peeled and coarsely grated
1 small Desiree potato, peeled and coarsely grated
1 banana shallot, peeled and thinly sliced (use a mandolin,
if you have one)
1 tbsp lemon juice
½ tsp each coriander seeds, celery seeds and caraway seeds,
toasted and finely crushed
½ garlic clove, peeled and crushed
2 eggs, beaten
2½ tbsp plain (all-purpose) flour
Vegetable oil, for frying
100g (3½oz) soured cream, to serve
Salt and freshly ground black pepper

For the salsa:
½ small shallot, peeled and very finely chopped
2 celery sticks, finely chopped
10g (¼oz) basil leaves, finely shredded
10g (¼oz) flat-leaf parsley, finely chopped
15g (½oz) capers, roughly chopped
Finely grated zest of 1 unwaxed lemon, plus 1 tbsp juice
1½ tbsp olive oil

Combine the celeriac, potato, shallot and lemon juice in a medium bowl with two teaspoons of salt, then tip into a sieve lined with a clean tea towel or cheesecloth. Set the sieve over a bowl and leave for 30 minutes for the liquid to drain off. Draw together the edges of the towel, then wring it a few times, to get rid of as much water as possible. Transfer to a clean bowl and combine with the spices, garlic, eggs and flour. Using your hands, form the mix into 10 patties, each about 6cm (2½in) wide, compressing the rösti as you make them, to squeeze out any remaining liquid.

Put all the salsa ingredients in a separate bowl, add a generous grind of pepper and mix to combine.

Pour enough oil into a medium-sized non-stick frying pan (skillet) to come 1.5cm (½in) up the sides. Put the pan on a medium heat and, once the oil is very hot, fry the rösti in batches for 7 minutes, turning them a few times, until crisp and golden-brown all over. Transfer to a plate lined with kitchen paper and keep warm while you cook the rest of the rösti. Serve at once with the salsa and a spoonful of soured cream.

SPICED BLUEBERRY MUFFIN CAKE
by Charlotte Druckman

This is a double hybrid: a cross between a muffin and a cake, and a mash-up of a blueberry bundt and a spiced breakfast pastry. Baking a giant muffin in a cast-iron frying pan creates what is, essentially, a giant top (the best part, as we all know). And if you've got all that surface area, you should do something special with it, such as brush it with melted butter and shower it with cinnamon sugar.

Serves 10 to 12

190g (6¾oz) plain (all-purpose) flour
100g (3½oz) granulated sugar
1½ tsp baking powder
½ tsp freshly grated nutmeg
¼ tsp salt
1 egg, lightly beaten
125ml (4fl oz) full-fat milk, at room temperature
1½ tsp vanilla extract
75g (2¾oz) unsalted butter, melted, slightly cooled, plus more
for the pan
340g (12oz) blueberries, fresh or frozen, half fork-crushed,
the rest left whole

For the topping:
35g (1¼oz) unsalted butter, melted
1 tbsp ground cinnamon
50g (1¾oz) granulated sugar

Place a 25cm (10in) cast-iron frying pan in the oven and preheat to 180°C/ 350°F/gas mark 4.

In a medium mixing bowl, stir together the flour, sugar, baking powder, nutmeg and salt. Make a well in the centre of the mixture.

In a smaller mixing bowl, stir together the egg, milk, vanilla and the melted butter. Stir in the mashed portion of the blueberries. Add this egg mixture to the flour mixture and stir until just moistened (don't worry if the batter is a little lumpy). Fold the whole blueberries into the batter.

Remove the hot pan from the oven, and carefully add a little butter (1–2 teaspoons should do) to melt, then brush it over the surface. Pour the batter into the hot pan. Bake in the oven for about 30 minutes or until a cake tester stuck in the centre comes out clean.

Meanwhile combine the cinnamon and sugar for the topping. Let the cake cool in the pan for 15 minutes before unmoulding it, carefully, while it's still warm, placing it on a plate set on a cooling rack.

For the topping, gradually brush the top of the cake with the melted butter, letting the butter soak in before adding more. Sprinkle the cinnamon-sugar mixture over the top.

Let the cake cool before serving. It's best eaten on the day it's baked. Have some for breakfast and then again for tea or an afternoon snack.

Reading List

Helena Attlee,
The Land Where Lemons Grow
A citrus-scented travelogue that brings the sweeping story of Italy and its cultural heritage vividly to life.

Alice Waters,
Chez Panisse Fruit
Exquisite sweet and savoury fruit recipes from the iconic Californian restaurant, and the best source for Meyer lemon ideas – try the crab salad with Meyer lemon, endive and watercress. Accompanied by stunning linocut prints by Patricia Curtan.

Deborah Levy,
Things I Don't Want to Know
The first in a series of 'living autobiographies' on writing and womanhood, and a powerful response to George Orwell's 1946 essay 'Why I Write'.

Signe Johansen, *Spirited*
Creative yet approachable drinks recipes informed by a cook's palate, from warming nightcaps and cocktails to smoothies and tonics.

Dave Broom,
The World Atlas of Whisky
The tome every whisky fan should own.

Rachel McCormack,
Chasing the Dram
Anecdotes, interviews, history and recipes that explore the importance of whisky in Scottish culture. Try the chocolate and whisky tiffin recipe.

Selina Nwulu,
The Secrets I Let Slip
A powerful and unflinching collection of poems that considers the beauty and pain of living in the modern world.

Marion Cunningham,
The Breakfast Book
A charming cookbook from the 1980s devoted to the first meal of the day, focusing on American favourites, such as pancakes, hash browns, muffins and all kinds of eggs.

Margaret Costa,
Four Seasons Cookery Book
A modern classic beloved of chefs and food writers. Flick to the wonderful chapter on comforting breakfasts and make the marmalade popovers.

Ella Risbridger,
Midnight Chicken
A moving account of the redemptive power of cooking, full of comforting recipes, such as roast garlic and tomato soup, spicy fish finger sandwiches and burnt-butter brownies.

Yotam Ottolenghi, *Simple*
Minimum hassle, maximum joy. An ode to the weeknight dinner, the low-key brunch and the one-pot wonder.

Charlotte Druckman, *Women on Food*
An unconventional anthology that brings together the radical, diverging female voices of the food industry.

February

THE COOK'S LARDER

Ingredients to look out for in February:

- Forced rhubarb, mandarins, pink grapefruit
- Chicory, flower sprouts, onions, puntarelle, savoy cabbage
- Bittercress, primroses
- Rabbit
- Coeur Neufchâtel, Comté

February feels motionless. Plants and animals are hibernating, winter veg is dwindling, stored produce is coming to an end and new growth has yet to appear. So it's time to take what remains, banish thoughts of frugality and cook something special. Claudia Roden says that 'true gastronomy is making the most of what is available, however modest'. Good advice for the month ahead.

Raid the store cupboard, add butter and cream and cheese to everything, bake cakes and pies and puddings; fortify yourself against winter's longueurs. Root vegetables are still here; try making the Swedish gratin-style dish Jansson's temptation. It's amazing what you can do with a few potatoes, a tin of anchovies and a glug of cream.

Take part in celebrations, even if they're not your own; gathering together to share food is never a bad idea. Join feasts for Chinese New Year — plump dumplings unveiled amid a plume of steam, platters of whole fish and roast pork, the soothing broth of Hainan chicken rice glistening with fat, sticky rice cakes and noodles slipping from chopsticks — or embrace the spirit of Mardi Gras with sweet rice fritters and puffed-up beignets covered in an avalanche of icing sugar. Valentine's Day is an excuse for good food too, whether you're dining solo, with friends or à deux. Love in all its forms deserves to be cherished.

Pancakes are the simplest and quickest of comfort foods, and are too good to enjoy solely on Shrove Tuesday. Risk a flip, then roll or fold: sticky fingers, messy mouth, the glee of endless toppings (although the classic combination of lemon and sugar is hard to beat). With a little determination, February can be fun.

Chinese Greens

AN ODE TO CHOI

The English expression 'eat your greens' sounds rather like an order to perform some faintly unpleasant duty. In China, greens of some sort, whether fresh or pickled, form part of almost every meal, and eating them is not a duty but a delight. It's partly the variety: numerous brassicas, the young sprouts of peas, pumpkins and other vegetables, water plants such as morning glory and water shield, medicinal weeds, mallows and vetches, to name just a few. It's also the delicate cooking. Leafy greens, when young and supple, are often chased around a hot wok at speed until just wilted but still bright and vibrant, or blanched fleetingly in boiling water.

Often, a plate of green vegetables is served as a gentle, refreshing counterpart to bolder dishes. Seasonings are minimal: perhaps just salt, garlic or ginger. Sometimes green leaves are briefly boiled and served in their cooking water with no flavourings at all as a palate cleanser, inviting appreciation of their *ben wei* or essential taste.

But Chinese greens can also dazzle. The Cantonese like to stir-fry water spinach with rich, funky fermented tofu and garlic. In southern Sichuan, blanched greens are served with spicy dipping sauces; using chopsticks to carry a strand of leaves towards the sauce is known as 'crossing the river'. Beijingers have a penchant for spinach soused in vinegar and tossed with fried peanuts. In other parts of China, you might enjoy cabbage stir-fried with dried shrimps, pork scratchings, fermented black beans or scorched chilli and Sichuan pepper. Chinese cooking tricks can transform familiar and seemingly mundane Western vegetables into something quite marvellous. Try stir-frying lettuce or steaming purple-sprouting broccoli and anointing it with salt and sesame oil.

WHAT TO DO WITH CHINESE GREENS

Chinese leaf cabbage
Stir-fry, pickle or boil in a good stock until
ribbony and tender.

Pak choi
Stir-fry with shiitake mushrooms
until juicy but still a little crisp.

Choy sum
Blanch and strew with slivers of ginger
and spring onion, then finish with a sizzle
of hot oil and a dash of light soy sauce.

Chinese broccoli or gai lan
Blanch until half-cooked, then stir-fry with finely
chopped ginger for a classic Cantonese taste.

Pea shoots or dou miao
Simply stir-fry with salt, or salt and minced garlic;
alternatively, add a few strands to a broth.

Water spinach or morning glory
Stir-fry with dried chilli and Sichuan
pepper or fermented tofu and garlic.

Chrysanthemum greens
Blanch, squeeze, season with salt
and sesame oil and serve as a salad.

Purple amaranth
Stir-fry with sliced garlic until the colour
runs from the purple leaves, creating a
magenta juice that pools in the dish.

The Kitchen God

by Fuchsia Dunlop

It was the twenty-third day of the last lunar month, and Mrs Zhou was showing me how to pay my respects to the Kitchen God. The red wooden tablet before me was inscribed with golden Chinese characters: 'The Kitchen God who determines our good fortune, *dingfu zao jun*.'

Mrs Zhou laid out a piece of loaf sugar in a small china dish and three incense sticks secured in a piece of carrot. We unwrapped the bundle of colourful printed paper offerings I'd bought for the occasion and placed them in a metal basin. Then Mrs Zhou lit the incense, set fire to the papers, which blazed up in bright, flickering flames, and taught me how to say my prayers: 'Thank you, Grandfather Kitchen God, for taking care of us this past year; please say a few good words about us to the Jade Emperor when you go up to Heaven; let us be safe and sound, well fed and clothed, this coming year.'

The Kitchen or Stove God, *zao jun*, is China's oldest and most intimate household god, a figure who grew out of the ancient worship of fire. Traditionally, he presides over the home from his perch above the kitchen range in the form of a statue, a wooden tablet or a wood-cut print. He's not really, as his name might suggest, the god of cooking, but rather a guardian and a watchman who keeps a keen eye on the family's behaviour from the hearth or the stove. Once a year, he is ceremonially dispatched to heaven to make his report – which is why people feed him with sweetmeats, to make his lips sticky and sweeten his words. He returns a week later to watch over the family and keep the peace for another year.

Despite his venerable age and roots in prehistory, the Kitchen God is a fading figure in modern China. In the remote countryside or temple shops you might still catch a glimpse of him, but in homes across most of the country, you're more likely to find images of the gods of wealth and longevity, Guanyin Buddha, or Mao Zedong. Not one among my Chinese friends has a Kitchen God in their homes, which is why they laugh to see my own statue, with his small offerings of fruit and incense. But I can't escape my fascination. I pursue the Kitchen God across China and in Chinatowns abroad, seeking out traditional shrines in old houses and museums. In an age of fast food and hurried lives, he's a reminder that the kitchen, the stove and the cooking fire are an inseparable part of what makes us human, and the heart of the home.

Taste of Carnival
by Lolis Eric Elie

I was born in New Orleans in 1963 and raised in that great city. When I think back to my childhood, one of my early cherished memories is of Carnival. When I was five or six years old, we would don costumes before sunrise on Carnival mornings and join other families on a decorated flatbed truck. We would drive around New Orleans throwing trinkets to the people we passed, blasting Carnival music from the truck's loudspeakers. These days Carnival is far more regulated and freelance floats are effectively barred.

Less than a dozen standard Carnival songs get played each year. 'Carnival Time' by Al Johnson has a particularly nostalgic pull for me. It's a reminder of the days when people in New Orleans spoke more often of 'Carnival' than of 'Mardi Gras'. Mardi Gras is the French name for the celebration and therefore is right at home in a city that was once a French colony. But the term Carnival connects the New Orleans celebration with similar fetes in the Caribbean and South America.

A few years ago I decided to host a Carnival party in those hazy afternoon hours after the parades had passed. The menu had to include meat since the whole idea is that Carnival is a carnivore's celebration in advance of the church-ordained abstinence of Lent. The star of the show was roast pork shoulder, stuffed with as many garlic cloves as I could fit, and braised slowly in the oven for ten hours on a bed of sliced onions.

Red beans and rice is the go-to dish for New Orleanians and our cousins in Haiti, but I wanted to do something a little different. I settled on the black beans favoured in Cuba and Brazil. Inspired by Austin Leslie, the New Orleans chef famed for his fried chicken and Creole-soul style of cooking, I created my own version of black beans and rum, using onions, garlic, oregano and olive oil to flavour the beans, along with the requisite rum. The combination spoke to my pan-Caribbean ambitions.

For dessert, I wanted to resuscitate a forgotten New Orleans dish: rice fritters, called 'calas', which are made with eggs, cooked rice, sugar and yeast. Unlike the city's signature beignets, calas were never commercially popular. They were sold on the streets, often by enslaved women, much as fried delicacies are sold on the streets of the Caribbean today.

When I told my mother I was making calas, she reminded me that Miriam Ortique, one of the women who rode the float with us, used to make calas on those early Carnival mornings. I smiled, realising that this effort to connect my city with the broader region surrounding it had also led me to reconnect with my own past.

Pancakes

In the 18th century, two variations on pancakes were popular: a 'rich man's' recipe and a 'poor man's' recipe. The poor man's pancakes were a simple assembly akin to the pancakes we still eat on Shrove Tuesday, although they were sometimes made with a mild ale rather than milk, and often fried in lard. Rich man's pancakes, made with the addition of cream, sherry, rose or orange flower water and grated nutmeg, sound indulgently delicious, and yet, as the food writer Jane Grigson points out, 'We have let it vanish from our tables and cling masochistically to the poor man's recipe'. The choice between the two was less to do with social standing, and more about how fancy you were feeling, with the more elaborate recipe often reserved for Sundays and feast days.

The recipe was sometimes called 'A Quire of Paper', meaning a stack of paper, which refers to the elegant, paper-thin pancakes it produces. Cookbooks of the time suggest they were piled high and cut like a cake. If you make them, serve the pancakes with nothing more than a sprinkle of sugar and perhaps a little lemon juice, or raid the dusty liqueur bottles at the back of the cupboard to make a Suzette sauce: caramelised sugar and butter, tangerine or orange juice, zest and orange liqueur, served flambéed for a theatrical flourish.

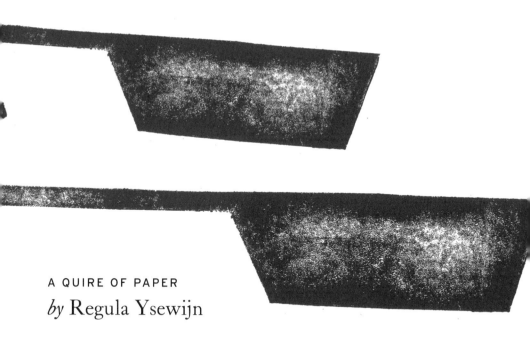

A QUIRE OF PAPER

by Regula Ysewijn

Makes a stack of 12

490g (1lb 1oz) plain (all-purpose) flour
1½ tsp grated nutmeg
2 tsp caster (superfine) sugar
300ml (10fl oz) double (heavy) cream
6 eggs plus 2 egg yolks
2 tsp orange flower water
120ml (4fl oz) sherry
200g (7oz) butter, plus extra for frying
Caster (superfine) sugar, to sprinkle in between layers

Combine the dry ingredients in a bowl and gradually add the cream, then the eggs, one at a time, including the extra yolks. When thoroughly combined, add the orange flower water and the sherry and whisk until smooth. Warm the butter until just melted, then pour into the batter and whisk until it is well incorporated.

Put a frying pan (skillet) or pancake pan over a high heat and let it get very hot. Add a little butter, pour in a spoonful of batter and let it spread as you turn the pan to guide the batter into shape. When it is golden on one side, place it on a plate, fried side down. Sprinkle with a little sugar. Repeat to make the rest of the pancakes, stacking them on top of each other and sprinkling the sugar before adding each new layer. If you make them thin enough, you should get 12 pancakes out of this batter. For a higher cake of 24 layers, simply double the recipe.

The Joy of Cooking for One

by Elisabeth Luard

A table for one is my kind of Valentine's Day love-in. Preferably at home with *The Best Exotic Marigold Hotel* on a loop, a glass of wine and a plateful of pata negra carved in short curls (*lonchas*) from the top of the haunch: the first velvety, buttery cut that comes to the knife when the ham is placed trotter-upwards in its cradle. You can tell pata negra – those salt-cured, wind-dried, cellar-matured hams of the semi-wild breed of Ibérico pig – by its elongated shape and slenderness of ankle. Serrano, prepared with the meat of grain-fed non-Ibéricos, is softer, bulkier and blander.

When the pigs are fed on acorns (*bellotas*), the meat is freckled with crystalline specks that form during lengthy cellaring, developing intensity of flavour in much the same way as wine matured in barrels. When carved in fine slivers with a frill of golden fat, the main source of the flavour, tradition dictates it should always be picked up and eaten with fingers, never with a knife and fork. So how do you tell if it's the real thing? It's easy, as José Gomez, a fifth-generation ham curer, explained to me one evening in a bar in Salamanca, a city famous for pata negra hams, 'Ibérico fat melts at blood temperature. Pick up your plateful and hold it sideways. If the ham sticks to the plate, it's pata negra. If it drops, ask for your money back.' I didn't put his method to the test – no sense in wasting good ham.

For me, Salamanca and its tapa bars bring back memories of journeys with my four young children when we lived in an Andalucían valley. Our home was rimmed by a cork-oak forest where Ibérico pigs foraged for acorns. Every year, advised and assisted by our self-sufficient neighbours, we kept a pig in a sty among the oaks to recycle the household scraps and provide the family with winter stores.

Back to my London kitchen, and bearing in mind that the proper conclusion of a Valentine's encounter is a leisurely morning-after, the last scraps of ham can be fried with eggs in a one-person *cazuela*, leaving the yolks soft enough for dipping with the last of the bread brushed with olive oil and toasted on a dry pan. And all for me, myself and I.

A Menu for February
by Lap-fai Lee

XO CHICKEN RICE

All Chinese New Year feasts should include a whole chicken. It symbolises the family and togetherness. The ultimate dish is Hainan Chicken Rice. I call my version 'XO Chicken Rice' or 'Seafood Treasure Chicken Rice' because I've upped the flavour with dried Cantonese seafood. The journey to ultimate chicken rice begins with good flavourful chicken. I like using Label Rouge corn-fed chicken from France. The French know how to breed chicken for maximum flavour but, best of all, they know to leave the massive plug of yellow chicken fat in the cavity. This is important because that chicken fat carries the essence of chicken. If you can't get hold of good chicken, an excellent substitute is guinea fowl.

```
For the chicken:
1 free-range corn-fed chicken, weighing about 1.5kg (3lb 5oz)
1 large thumb-sized piece of fresh ginger, lightly bashed
3 large spring onions (scallions)
Salt
```

Remove the plug of fat from the cavity of the chicken and set aside for cooking the rice. If you need more fat, trim off any excess skin.

In a pan that is just larger than the chicken, boil enough water to barely submerge the bird. Add the ginger, spring onions and plenty of salt. Taste the water for saltiness as this will eventually be used to cook the rice. The water should be as salty as pasta water – as salty as the sea.

Lower the chicken gently into the boiling water, dipping it several times breast-side down, so that the skin tightens and won't split during cooking. Lay the chicken breast-side up in the pan and bring the water back up to a simmer. Cover and simmer gently for 15 minutes, then turn off the heat and let it finish cooking in the residual heat for a further 40 minutes. Adjust the time if you have a larger chicken. You are looking for an internal (inside thigh) temperature of no more than 70°C/158°F. Keep the chicken stock to cook the rice.

Plunge the bird in a large bowl of iced water and leave it there to chill for 10 minutes. This will stop the cooking and keep the chicken succulent.

Carefully hang the bird upside down for at least an hour to bring it back up to room temperature and for the flavour to fully develop. The chilling will produce a flavourful layer of chicken jelly in between the skin and meat, which is the sign of great poached chicken.

```
For the rice:
40g (1½oz) chicken fat
150g (5½oz) shallots, finely sliced
1 large garlic clove, minced
450g (1lb) jasmine rice, washed and drained
80g (3oz) dried scallops and prawns soaked in cold water until soft
(at least 6 hours)
2 pandan leaves, split and tied into a knot
5cm (2in) square of kombu
```

In a large saucepan, warm the chicken fat over a low heat until it renders. Add the shallots and slowly fry for 15 minutes until they are brown and sticky – be careful not to burn them.

Add the garlic and cook briefly to take the rawness out of it before adding the reserved chicken stock (from the poached chicken) and the water used to soak the dried seafood. You now have your flavoured chicken stock with which to cook your rice.

Add the rice to the stock. Shred or chop the seafood into small pieces and add to the rice, along with the pandan leaves and kombu.

Cook the rice using the absorption method (I transfer the whole lot to a rice cooker) with roughly 1.25 parts stock to 1 part rice by volume. If you regularly cook white rice by the absorption method, allow a little extra stock to compensate for the additional seafood in the pot. Once the rice is cooked, serve the chicken neatly sliced and devour with ginger and spring onion oil.

GINGER AND SPRING ONION OIL

```
70g (2½oz) fresh ginger, finely grated
35g (1¼oz) spring onions (scallions), equal white and green parts,
finely chopped
15g (½oz) fresh coriander (cilantro), mostly stalks, finely chopped
1 tsp salt
5 tbsp groundnut (peanut) or vegetable oil
Soy sauce
```

Combine the ginger, spring onions, coriander and salt in a heatproof bowl.

Heat the oil in a small pan over a hight heat until it is smoking. Using a chopstick, make little wells in your ginger mixture and pour the smoking oil all over it. It will sizzle – lots. The little wells will ensure the hot oil reaches all the nooks. The mixture should be a runny, oily paste consistency. If it isn't, sizzle some more oil into it. Finish with the merest dash of soy sauce to round off the flavour.

BRAISED SHIITAKE, TOFU AND CHAI CHOI

Chai choi is a traditional braised vegetarian dish that's eaten on festival days by those practising Buddhism. This is a delicious medley of ingredients, full of sweet umami and comforting flavours.

```
Groundnut (peanut) or vegetable oil, for frying
2 spring onions (scallions), finely chopped, whites and greens
separated
3 slices of fresh ginger
2 garlic cloves, lightly crushed
6 large shiitake mushrooms, soaked until soft, stems removed and
quartered, soaking liquor reserved
A splash of Shaoxing wine
2 sticks of tofu skin, soaked until soft, cut into 4cm (1½in) pieces
Small handful of dried lily flowers, soaked until soft
8 small cubes of deep-fried tofu
2 fingers' worth of black sea moss
2 small cubes of fermented tofu, mashed into a paste
1 tbsp soy sauce
1 tbsp oyster sauce
25g (1oz) yellow miso paste
20g (¾oz) caster (superfine) sugar
```

In a large frying pan (skillet), add the oil and fry the spring onion whites, ginger and garlic to release the aroma. Add the mushrooms and splash in the Shaoxing wine to sizzle off the alcohol. Add all of the other ingredients and top up with the soaking liquor from the mushrooms. There should be enough liquid to gently braise the ingredients together for 30 minutes. Garnish with the spring onion greens before serving.

Reading List

Hsiang Ju Lin,
Slippery Noodles
A culinary history of China, covering topics as diverse as the influence of the Silk Road, health food in the 16th century and the lavish banquets of the Mongol court.

Fuchsia Dunlop,
The Food of Sichuan
An impressive tome, detailed and captivating, that extols the charms of fish-fragrant aubergine, mapo tofu and the lip-tingling thrill of Sichuan pepper.

Lolis Eric Elie, *Treme*
Stories, recipes, history and lore from the heart of New Orleans, based on the HBO series of the same name.

The Picayune,
The Picayune's Creole Cook Book
First published in 1901 by a New Orleans newspaper determined to preserve the rich tradition of Creole cooking, this classic cookbook is still the bible of Louisiana cuisine.

Regula Ysewijn,
Pride and Pudding
A homage to the great British puddings of the past with recipes for the 21st century.

Elisabeth Luard,
The Flavours of Andalucía
A culinary survey of the eight provinces of Andalucía, laced with personal narrative and beautiful watercolours by the author.

Katharine Whitehorn,
Cooking in a Bedsitter
The 1960s kitchen classic for solo diners written by the domestic goddess who couldn't cook. Recipe cooking times do not include 'the time it takes you to find the salt in the suitcase under the bed'.

Laura Esquivel,
Like Water for Chocolate
A sumptuous feast of a novel, full of romance, tragedy and the magic of food. Take it into the kitchen to cook the Mexican recipes that begin each chapter.

March

THE COOK'S LARDER

Ingredients to look out for in March:

- Purple sprouting broccoli, spring greens, spring onions
- Alexanders, birch sap, chickweed, dandelion leaves, nettles, sea kale, wild garlic
- Fleur du Maquis, Pecorino Sardo

The start of spring — stirrings — hope. Fierce bright leaves shoot up towards the strengthening sun, defying the harshest weather. On a clear day, head out to pick nettles, wild garlic and alexanders from the woods and hedgerows. This may sound a little whimsical, like something out of an Enid Blyton novel, but foraging in early spring has a practical edge: wild plants steal a march on their cultivated cousins, and it's a joyful yearly reminder, after the store-cupboard reliance of winter, that food tastes best when freshly picked and in season.

March is the best time of year for tapping trees and collecting the sap. If you're feeling adventurous, find a silver birch tree, drill a hole and boil down the bounty to make syrup. A more realistic option is to buy good quality maple syrup. Thanks to its sugary shelf life, we rarely think of it as a seasonal treat, but sap boilers are now bubbling away in the wilds of Canada, sending billowing clouds of sweet maple-scented steam into the air.

Despite the first spirit-lifting signs of spring, we're still in need of comfort and familiarity on the plate. Bake or buy a sturdy sourdough and look to good things on toast for simple suppers. Welsh rarebit is a dish to confront a cold snap — a 'noble version of cheesy toast' according to the chef Fergus Henderson — with the fortifying additions of mustard, stout and Worcestershire sauce. It's best eaten, as Henderson suggests, 'when bubbling golden brown... washed down with a glass of port'.

Wild Garlic

A PUNGENT WOODLAND WALK

The Dorset naturalist John Wright notes in his excellent handbook, *The Forager's Calendar*, 'If there is one species that stirs the heart of all foragers, it must be wild garlic… one of the most giving of all wild foods.' Indeed, it's one of the easiest plants to forage and can even be found in towns and cities – pungent clusters congregating under the damp shade of old trees, tufts of green sprouting next to forgotten gravestones and park benches.

If you come across swathes of wild garlic on a woodland walk, it will be your nose that discovers them first. The broad, spear-shaped leaves are easy to identify; a few plants, such as the poisonous lily of the valley, look superficially alike, but none have wild garlic's characterful smell. The taste and aroma is reminiscent of chives, spring onions and, of course, garlic – a strong flavour that mellows when cooked.

Wild garlic can be picked with abandon. The season is long and the leaves are both abundant and versatile, but early spring is the time to gorge: the leaves are fully grown and at their most succulent but have yet to acquire the bitter intensity of later plants. From late April until June you'll also find pretty white flowers and seed pods to add a subtle garlic punch to salads and soups.

WHAT TO DO WITH WILD GARLIC

- Make a pesto using walnuts instead of pine nuts.
- Add to an omelette or scrambled eggs.
- Mix with ricotta, Parmesan and a little nutmeg to make a filling for ravioli.
- Stir into risottos or add to spring broths.
- Toss with boiled potatoes when they're still steaming from the pan.
- Whip up a wild garlic mayonnaise using cold-pressed rapeseed oil.
- Stuff into the cavity of a whole fish or chicken with slices of lemon and fresh thyme.
- Later in the season, tempura the flowers and pickle the pods.

THE DEVIL'S POSY

Wild garlic has many colloquial names, the most hostile of which come from Somerset and Dorset: devil's posy, stinking Jenny, snake's food and onion stinkers. In continental Europe, the bulbs are thought to be a favourite food of brown bears, hence the plant's botanical name, *Allium ursinum* (bear leek).

Where the Wild Things Are

SPRING FORAGING

HOP SHOOTS

The hop plant is best known for its use in making beer, but in early spring it's worth looking for its fine shoots in the tangled hedgerows. Pick the tips of the vine before the leaves unfurl, when they look like miniature asparagus. Blanch in salted water and serve with melted butter or hollandaise. Add to salads, omelettes and risottos, or sauté with mushrooms and serve on toast.

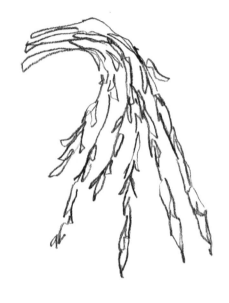

NETTLES

Instantly recognisable by their ragged leaves, these weeds are so common they can be picked in heroic quantities. Wear thick gloves to gather the youngest leaves, which lose their sting once blanched. Nettle soup is the classic dish, thickened with potato or celeriac, but reserve some of the cooked leaves to purée and add to frittatas or buttery mashed potato. Sandwich between garlic-rubbed bread with plenty of herbs and mozzarella for an unexpectedly delicious toastie.

GORSE FLOWERS

On a sunny day, the scent of coconut will draw you to these bright yellow flowers. This evergreen shrub is common in coastal areas and on heathland but can grow almost anywhere. Pick carefully to avoid its sharp spines. The ephemeral scent of the flowers can be captured in vinegar, vodka or wine, although a simple syrup is perhaps the most useful infusion.

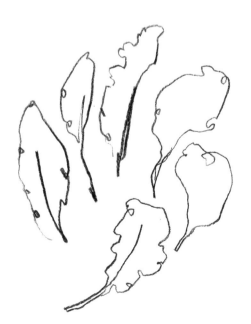

SEA KALE

A maritime plant that can grow to a monstrous size on shingle beaches, sea kale is best picked young – like most foraged leaves. It has been cooked for kings and presidents – Thomas Jefferson grew the plant in his garden – and Jane Grigson refers to it as 'an aristocrat of the northern coasts'. If the shoots are young and tender, eat them raw; if they're a little tough, simply fry them in olive oil until crisp.

Maple Syrup
by Simon Thibault

As a child in Nova Scotia, I thought that everyone experienced the start of spring in the same way I did: it was the sound of boots crunching through iced snow banks; it smelled of pine and cedar and maple and woodsmoke all at once. And most of all, it felt warm and dewy on your face from the steam billowing out of an old sap boiler.

My family and I spent many a winter evening in the woodland home of our friends, Clément and Rose. The house was powered by a water wheel and a generator, fed and warmed by a wood-burning stove. And when winter and spring abutted in March, we would spend time in their *cabane à sucre*, or sugar shack.

In Eastern Canada the force of sap rising from the roots of maple trees is nature's message that spring is coming. Traditionally, this syrup was collected drop by drop in buckets nailed to trees, but today it travels along a network of pipes through the woods, arriving at the cabanes that can be found throughout this part of the country.

There was enough room in the cabane for Clément, my mother and father, my sister and I, and the sap boiler smack-dab in the middle. Tin cups hung on weathered nails by the doorway, waiting for you to pick them up and take a sip of the slowly reducing sap. Those first sips are akin to drinking winter sun in liquid form, while sitting in a cedar-lined sauna. Later in the day, it will taste almost vegetal, like munching on pea pods while sipping barley tea. As time passes, the liquor deepens in colour and character, with twenty litres of sap becoming just one litre of syrup. That bubbling brew changes not only with the time of day, but the time of year: early batches will be paler and softer in character than their malty late-season counterparts.

While waiting for the sap to transform, we would return to the house, where Rose would be tending to her wood-burning stove. There she would stir the contents of an enamel pot, cooking down the maple syrup into butter. She knew by intimation and habit how much wood was needed to stoke the fire, and what it would smell like when the liquid started to crystallise, churning itself into maple cream and eventually becoming maple butter. This she would do while tending to the pot of beans that sat on the back half of the stove, supper for that night.

Clément and Rose are gone now, but their cabane and home still stand in the woods of southwestern Nova Scotia, tended and used by their son. My winters are never far away from wood-burning stoves, or enamel cups, and the sound of boots crunching through snow banks, on my way to sweetness.

On Toast
by Marina O'Loughlin

Toast has been a constant source of comfort and pleasure throughout my life. As a restaurant critic, my weeks are punctuated by elaborate tasting menus, ambitious restaurants with their lacto-fermentation and vegetable desserts, and nouveau street food markets with their 'slutty' and 'dirty' offerings – handheld collisions of salts and sugars and fats. I'm not deprived of culinary stimulation.

But what do I eat when not on the job? Left to my own devices, it's toast in front of the TV – no competition. Toast: that little word contains galaxies. What kind of bread? Nutty wholegrain, dense-crusted sourdough, fat blowsy sliced white, ciabatta, focaccia, rye, baguette, bloomer? Do we count the likes of crumpets and English muffins? (I do.) Then there's what you can do with it: pile it up with buttery scrambled eggs; mature Cheddar cheese with Colman's English mustard, blasted under the grill until bubbling; creamy, tarragon-spiked mushrooms; or pile high with deli buys – salumi and charcuterie, hams and cheeses, roasted peppers and crisp, vinegary onions. Bloody avocado.

I self-medicate with toast when I'm ill, celebrate with it when I'm happy, crave it when I'm low. To me, the three loveliest words in the English language aren't 'I love you' but 'hot buttered toast'. When feeling peaky as kids, it wasn't pasta my Italian mother gave us, but chopped-up boiled eggs with salt and butter – 'egg in a cup' – and triangles of white toast. This still tastes like love to me. In his food memoir, *Toast*, Nigel Slater says, 'It's impossible not to love someone who makes toast for you.' I agree. I think my most miserable times coincided with various low-carb diets: everything seemed so much gloomier and less easy to handle without the fortification of toast.

I was once asked to choose my last meal and the answer was easy: I said I'd like the thick, lumpy 'heels' of a Scottish plain loaf, those curious rectangular-oblong jobs with a crust only at either end, toasted and spread with so much salted butter that it created glossy pools. I added a side order of MDMA – well, if I'm about to croak, I might as well go out cheerful – but if I had to choose with a gun to my head, I could lose that bit. For me, the toast is what's important. Always, always toast.

Excellent Things on Toast

SAVOURY

- Lots of very good salted butter
- Butter and tomatoes with sea salt
- Eggs and/or smoked fish of any kind
- Wild mushrooms with garlic and thyme
- Welsh rarebit
- Crushed peas, lemon and mint
- Cold butter and Cantabrian anchovies
- Roast bone marrow
- Mashed potato

SWEET

- Salted butter and honey
- Cinnamon sugar
- Any jam made by a friend
- Peanut butter, honey and banana
- Tahini and grape molasses
- Ricotta and figs, peaches or berries
- Dark chocolate ganache, sea salt and olive oil
- Chestnut paste
- Condensed milk
- Kaya (coconut jam)

Savouries

Savouries are peculiar to the British. A delicious salty morsel at the end of a meal was a popular addition to the menu during Victorian and Edwardian times, although the savoury course gradually fell out of fashion and is now a nostalgic rarity. In his 1934 recipe collection *Good Savouries*, Ambrose Heath insisted that the savoury 'makes an admirable ending to a meal, like some unexpected witticism or amusing epigram at the end of a pleasant conversation'. Modest portions of Welsh rarebit (or rabbit), Scotch woodcock, angels on horseback and devilled kidneys were brought to the table, invariably served on toast. Cheese, eggs and anchovies often featured. The common theme: robustly seasoned dishes with an umami kick, leading to more bottles of wine or port being opened so the night could march on. Could it be time for a revival?

A Menu for March
by Anna Jones

WILD GARLIC AND PUY LENTIL SOUP

In wild garlic season, I pick loads and make it into a pesto, which can be kept under a slick of olive oil in the fridge for weeks or in the freezer for much longer. Wild garlic has a strong taste when it's raw, which mellows when you cook it. If you can't get your hands on it, a finely chopped clove of garlic and some spinach will stand in.

```
Serves 4

200g (7oz) dried Puy lentils
Good olive oil
1 banana shallot, finely chopped
1 fennel bulb, finely chopped
2 sticks of celery, finely chopped
50g (1¾oz) swede (rutabaga), parsnip or carrot, finely chopped
50g (1¾oz) hazelnuts
1 unwaxed lemon
50g (1¾oz) wild garlic
50g (1¾oz) young spinach or other greens
```

First soak the lentils in boiling water for 10 minutes; this will help speed up the cooking time and make them softer. Drain the lentils and put them into a large, deep saucepan with 750ml (1¼ pints) of cold water and simmer until they are cooked and soft but not falling apart – this should take 20–25 minutes.

Put another pan over a medium heat, add a little oil and the shallot, fennel, celery and your root vegetable. Add a good pinch of salt, then cook for 10 minutes, until soft and sweet.

Meanwhile, toast the hazelnuts in a dry pan until golden brown. Once they are nicely toasted, take off the heat. Grate in the lemon zest and add 2 tablespoons of olive oil, then put the pan back on the heat for a minute or so until you hear a sizzle. Transfer the lot to a bowl to cool. Once cool, roughly chop.

Fill and boil the kettle. Once the vegetables and the lentils are both cooked, stir the vegetables into the lentils and add 500ml (18fl oz) of hot water from the kettle. Leave to simmer on a very low heat.

Put the wild garlic into a bowl, cover with boiling water and leave for a minute, then scoop out with a slotted spoon. Squeeze out any excess water, then put into a food processor with a tablespoon of oil and enough cold water (about 2 tablespoons) to purée it. Stir the spinach and wild garlic purée through the soup. Serve with the lemony hazelnuts, a little more olive oil and wild garlic flowers, if you have them.

CRUSHED NEW POTATOES, PURPLE SPROUTING BROCCOLI AND BLOOD ORANGE CREAM

This is a gentle, soothing dish. The potatoes are warm, crisp and golden next to the bright broccoli stems, whose little tree-tops soak up the pale-pink blood orange cream. I eat this for supper but also often serve it as part of a spread, as its subtle notes mean it goes well with an endless list of things.

Serves 4

600g (1lb 5oz) new potatoes, large ones halved
300g (10½oz) purple sprouting broccoli
2 tbsp olive oil
2 garlic cloves, skin on
150g (5½oz) crème fraîche
Zest and juice of 2 unwaxed blood oranges
50g (1¾oz) hazelnuts
Salt and freshly ground black pepper

Put the potatoes into a medium saucepan and cover with cold water. Add a generous pinch of salt and bring to the boil over a high heat. Once the potatoes are boiling, let them cook for a further 10–12 minutes, depending on the size, until a knife passes through them easily.

While the potatoes are cooking, trim the broccoli spears, nicking off any dry, tough ends and slicing any larger pieces in half lengthways.

Remove the potatoes with a slotted spoon, leaving the pan on the heat. Place them in a bowl and cover to keep warm. Lower the broccoli into the water in which the potatoes were cooking and boil for 3–4 minutes, until just tender. Leave to steam dry.

Find two frying pans (skillets) whereby one fits inside the other easily and heat the olive oil in the larger one over a medium heat (if you don't have two frying pans you could just roast the potatoes in the oven, at 220°C/425°F/gas mark 7, at the beginning of the recipe and burst a few with a potato masher halfway through). Bash the garlic cloves with the side of a knife and put them into the hot oil, leave for a minute to flavour the oil, then take the garlic out and put to one side. Place the potatoes in the pan and cover with the smaller pan so that the potatoes are crushed by the weight of the pan. Cook the potatoes like this for 25 minutes, turning them 2–3 times during the cooking process and pressing down with the back of a wooden spoon on some to help them split and crisp.

Meanwhile, mix the crème fraîche with the blood orange zest and juice and season with salt and pepper. Toast your hazelnuts quickly in a dry pan over a medium heat until they turn from pale brown to a rich golden brown, then remove and roughly chop.

Once the potatoes are crisp, split and golden, tip them out of the pan into a serving bowl and put the pan back on the heat. Peel and roughly chop the cooked garlic and add it to the pan with the broccoli. Cook until the edges of the broccoli begin to crisp – this should take only a few minutes.

Tumble the broccoli into the bowl, top with the blood orange crème fraîche and mix while everything is still warm. Scatter over the hazelnuts and serve in the middle of the table.

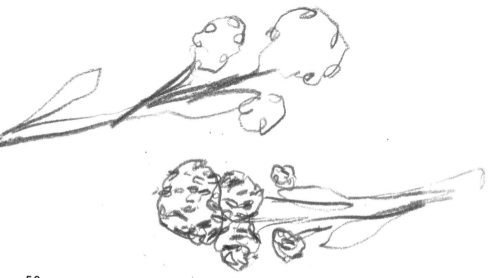

LEMON AND CARDAMOM UPSIDE-DOWN CAKE

For me, there is no greater cake than a lemon cake, and this one takes the crown.
It's an upside-down cake with an easy candied lemon bottom, which, once cool, is
turned out to become a gilded lemon roof. The lemons burnish as the cake cooks,
under a crumb of almonds, polenta and oats. The lemon comes with a back-up of
cardamom and vanilla, a combination that's well used in my kitchen.

```
Serves 10

Butter, for greasing
5 unwaxed lemons
175g (6oz) golden caster (superfine) sugar
75g (2½oz) rolled oats
Seeds from 12 cardamom pods
150ml (5fl oz) rapeseed oil
75g (2½oz) fine polenta (cornmeal)
1 tsp baking powder
75g (2½oz) ground almonds
1 tsp vanilla paste
3 eggs
Generous pinch of flaky sea salt
Plain yogurt whipped with a little vanilla, to serve
```

Preheat your oven to 200°C/400°F/gas mark 6. Next, grease and line a 24cm
(9½in) springform cake tin with baking paper.

Put the zest and juice of 2 of the lemons into a small bowl and set aside. Next, prepare the remaining lemons for the base of the tin. Using a really sharp knife, slice the lemons into wafer-thin slices, about 0.5cm (¼in) is ideal. Remove any visible pips from the slices.

Put 50g (1¾oz) of the sugar into a medium saucepan with 50ml (3½ tbsp) of water and heat until the sugar has dissolved, then simmer for about 5 minutes until you have a syrup. Add the lemon slices and very gently simmer for another 10–15 minutes until they are starting to turn slightly translucent, then carefully scoop them out of the syrup and put them on to some baking paper to cool so that you can handle them. Reserve any syrup for later.

Meanwhile, blitz the oats in the food processor until you have a rough, flour-like consistency.

Bash the cardamom seeds to a rough powder. Beat together the rapeseed oil and remaining sugar with a wooden spoon. Mix in the polenta, baking powder, almonds, cardamom, vanilla, eggs, ground oats and reserved lemon juice and zest. Sprinkle over the salt and mix well again.

Arrange the sliced citrus on the bottom of the lined cake tin, leaving some little gaps for the batter to hit the bottom of the tin, which will allow some of the steam to escape. Pour the batter on top and level it out with the back of a spoon.

Bake in the middle of the oven for 35–40 minutes, checking at 30 minutes and perhaps covering with foil if it looks as if it's getting very brown on top. Check that it's cooked through by piercing the cake with a skewer; if it comes out clean, the cake is ready.

Let it cool for about 20 minutes, then remove the tin, peel away the paper and carefully upturn it on to a plate. Pour any leftover syrup from the lemons over the top. Serve with yogurt, whipped with a little vanilla.

Reading List

Roger Phillips, *Wild Food*
A guide to foraging in woods and fields, and along river banks, seashores and moors, with useful colour photography and detailed descriptions for accurate identification.

Simon Thibault, *Pantry and Palate*
A family narrative that spans over a hundred years, remembering and rediscovering Acadian food through recipes and traditions.

Marie Nightingale, *Out of Old Nova Scotia Kitchens*
First published in 1970 and still popular today, this was one of the first books to look at the cuisine of Nova Scotia, recognising the cultural and culinary contributions of indigenous and colonial residents.

Nigel Slater, *Toast*
An intimate story of a childhood remembered through food that begins with burnt toast and ends with profiteroles and hot chocolate sauce.

Fergus Henderson and Trevor Gulliver, *The Book of St John*
Part food gospel, part memoir, part recipe book celebrating 25 years of the world-famous English restaurant. Excellent ideas for things on toast and other simple pleasures: a bacon sandwich and a glass of cider; a doughnut and a flute of champagne.

Ambrose Heath, *Good Savouries*
An entire book, published in 1934, devoted to the lost tradition of savouries.

Anna Jones, *The Modern Cook's Year*
Vegetarian recipes arranged in rhythm with nature, interspersed with seasonal playlists, foraging tips and flowers to look out for each month.

April

THE COOK'S LARDER

Ingredients to look out for in April:

- Outdoor rhubarb
- Asparagus, morels, radish, sorrel, watercress
- Dandelion flowers, gorse, hop shoots,
  rock samphire, sea spinach, wild fennel
- Wood pigeon
- Wigmore, Valençay

Wordsworth's dancing daffodils, spring showers, the soft and ephemeral snow of blossoms — April is all about change. Smart bundles of asparagus herald the start of the year's fresh produce bounty. Traditionally, the asparagus season runs from St George's Day on 23 April — he is the patron saint of farmers after all — through to the summer solstice. A fleeting seasonal treat.

Spring sparks a longing for sharper, sprightlier flavours. Outdoor rhubarb is the only fruit (although technically a vegetable) in season, so make the most of it in crumbles, pies, trifles and fools, or perhaps a cocktail, tart and pretty, garnished with a fresh stick to stir. It may not be as eye-catching or sweet-tasting as the early forced variety, but it is perfect for rounding off a spring dinner party, especially if the meal has been a rich one.

To further celebrate the vivifying effect of sour, look to sorrel, a herb that flourishes early and certainly deserves more attention than it receives. Valued for its sharpness in the days before lemons, it can be used as both herb and vegetable, its lively, refreshing tang lending itself to egg and seafood dishes. Jane Grigson, lamenting our constant desire for novelty, once used the neglect of sorrel as an example of our fickle nature. 'We are so busy running after the latest dish,' she observed in 1974, 'that the good things we've known for centuries are forgotten as quickly as the boring ones.'

Not all culinary traditions are forgotten so easily. Sweet breads are still baked throughout Europe at Easter: tsoureki in Greece, colomba in Italy, paska in Slovakia and hot cross buns in Britain. Even if we're distracted by the hunt for chocolate eggs, there's always time for tea and cake.

Saffron

GOLDEN YEARS

Saffron must be used with caution. Its earthy, honeyed aroma and warm, slightly bitter taste can take on an astringent, almost medicinal quality if the pinch is too generous. Just a few strands – Claudia Roden advises counting five or six per serving – lends a delicious quality and striking golden hue to dishes, such as paella, biryani, bouillabaisse and risotto alla milanese.

This ancient spice has long been held in great esteem. It features in the Greek myth of Crocus and Smilax and was used as a ritual offering to deities in ancient Persia. It is often talked of as being the most expensive spice in the world, worth more per gram than gold. This is true, due to the painstaking way it is produced. The pale-purple flowers of *Crocus sativus* are harvested by hand at dawn, and the three delicate stigmas are removed and carefully dried. Two hundred flowers yield just one gram of saffron.

Saffron came to England in the 14th century and flourished along the east coast for hundreds of years before gradually dying out. This heritage can be found in place names such as Saffron Walden, the Essex town at the centre of English saffron production during Tudor times. In recent years, a handful of pioneering farmers have revived the lost art of saffron growing. Essex farmer David Smale ages his saffron for up to a year, a practice that mellows some of the high notes and results in a more complex flavour. He recommends gently crushing the spice in a pestle and mortar before soaking it in warm water overnight to extract the vibrant colour and elusive flavour. Throwing it into the cooking pot at the last moment is an expensive folly.

Saffron has long been associated with Easter and Christmas festivities. In her seminal *Four Seasons Cookery Book*, Margaret Costa relates that the traditional Easter simnel cake used to be 'cooked with a crocus-yellow crust of saffron bread over its "marchpane" top' and eaten with mulled ale. Like many traditions around feast days, the recipe has been forgotten, but saffron cakes are still eaten in Cornwall on Good Friday, served with a generous dollop of clotted cream.

Matzo Balls
by Erica Wagner

Matzo meal, eggs, schmaltz, salt, pepper, finely chopped parsley. These are the simple ingredients for matzo balls, the traditional accompaniment for Jewish chicken soup. Schmaltz, for those unfamiliar, is chicken fat, which I save from the bottom of a pan. When I trim chicken thighs of extra skin I render the little snippets and pour the rich liquid into a jar. (Those rendered snips can be salted to make *gribenes*, another Yiddish word, and yummy they are too.) These days I add a pinch of baking powder to my matzo balls: I discovered the trick on the food blog of culinary historian Tori Avey. No, baking powder isn't kosher for Passover, but my Jewishness is more cultural than practical, so in it goes: the resulting matzo balls are veritably cloud-like in their lightness.

I wish I could tell my mother about the baking powder; she's been gone ten years now. She didn't love to cook, but she was proud of her matzo balls, viewing them as a constant work-in-progress. To her, the ideal matzo ball was always just out of reach, floating serenely in a bowl of perfectly golden chicken broth. Another thing I never got to tell her is that I add turmeric to my broth these days, to bring out an even deeper gold. There's no mention of turmeric in Julia Moskin's excellent recipe for chicken soup on the *New York Times* cooking website, and I have no recollection of where I discovered this trick, but I'll share it with you as I will share my bowl of soup.

Chicken soup with matzo balls is surely the ultimate food of comfort and welcome: delicate and fragrant, perfect for springtime – and yet, of course, equally gratifying in the depths of winter. To make it from scratch is a couple of days' easy work. When it's time for me to take the matzo mix and begin to form it into dumplings – a little less than half the size of a ping-pong ball, I'd say, as they swell while they cook – I think of my mother. Ten years gone: but we are together here at the stove, still. The schmaltz slicks my palms – I'm thinking that soon my son will be home to eat a bowl of my chicken soup; and there is my mother, in my memory, her palms slicked with schmaltz, making chicken soup for me.

Eggs

Eggs are mysterious and miraculous. Delicate, pleasing to hold, satisfying in their completeness. They are the ultimate fast food, and the foundation for the simplest of meals and the greatest of culinary creations.

Many great writers have paid tribute to the egg. The French philosopher Diderot famously pronounced that all the world's theologies could be toppled by one. And the infinitely quotable M.F.K. Fisher wrote that 'one of the most private things in the world is an egg before it is broken'.

Jane Grigson had particularly firm opinions on the matter of cooking eggs: 'Egg dishes should be nothing if not a combination of simplicity, purity, flavour and richness,' she said. She was much taken by the novelist Henry James's description of 'an excellent repast' in Bourg-en-Bresse which, he wrote, 'consisted simply of boiled eggs and bread and butter. It was the quality of these simple ingredients that made the occasion memorable.'

Simplicity is key, but everyone has their own tips and tricks, and their own idea of perfection. The American cookbook author James Beard asserted, 'There are few things as magnificent as scrambled eggs, pure and simple, perfectly cooked and perfectly seasoned.' He would add a dash of Tabasco and whisk in a little water for lightness. Julia Child championed the method of first simmering eggs in their shells for a few seconds to achieve the perfect poached egg; and Margaret Costa suggested frying eggs 'very slowly in butter, or butter and bacon fat, spooning the butter over them to firm the yolk'.

Elizabeth David wrote often about omelettes – an 'almost primitive and elemental meal' – favouring the classic *omelette aux fines herbes*, which she memorably described as 'something gentle and pastoral, with the clean scent of the dairy, the kitchen garden, the basket of early morning mushrooms or the sharp tang of freshly picked herbs'. Years later, the screenwriter Nora Ephron waged war against the tasteless egg-white omelette that had become ubiquitous in the US: 'This is my moment to say what's been in my heart for years: it's time to put a halt to the egg-white omelette.'

Diana Henry writes: 'A pleasing lunch is a warm boiled egg broken up with a fork, seasoned, drizzled with olive oil, with tomatoes or purple-sprouting alongside.' Indeed, an egg can turn anything into a meal: beat with Parmesan and drizzle into broth to make an Italian soup called *stracciatella*; gently poach and serve atop spring greens or asparagus; fry in oil and flop, sizzling and netted with brown, on rice, noodles or any kind of hash – eggs are the queens of leftovers. If in doubt, put an egg on it.

GOOD THINGS TO DO WITH EGGS

Mimosa
The name given to dishes garnished with hard-boiled egg yolks, reminiscent of mimosa flowers scattered over snow. Push the yolks through a coarse sieve and sprinkle over asparagus, salads or leeks vinaigrette.

Huevos con puntilla
To achieve crispy edges – or 'eggs with a frilly lace hem' – chef José Pizarro recommends using a small pan and heating olive oil until it just starts to smoke. The egg will splutter and sizzle, and is particularly good served with asparagus and Serrano ham.

A fricassee of eggs
A recipe from the 18th-century cookery writer Hannah Glasse. Boil eggs for 8 minutes, then shell and quarter them. Reduce butter and cream 'till it is thick and smooth', pour over the eggs and serve with toast.

Cold omelette with vinaigrette
When making an omelette, Nigel Slater recommends making a second one and keeping it in the fridge for the next day: 'It will come to little harm overnight, then eat it cold, with a strong chive dressing.'

Kuku sabzi
The Persian answer to frittata, according to chef Samin Nosrat. Use just enough egg to bind together the herbs and greens (try chard, coriander and dill). Cook like a frittata and serve with feta cheese, yogurt or pickles.

Anzacs
by Kate Young

During my teenage years, my parents would wake me at four in the morning every 25 April. My sister and I were part of our school choir in Brisbane, a gaggle of teenage girls in navy blazers and white socks, and we sang each year in remembrance at the Anzac Day dawn service. On our way home, despite the early hour, we munched on Anzac biscuits – only fair, we reasoned, given how long we had been awake.

An annual holiday in Australia, Anzac Day commemorates the landing of the Australia and New Zealand Army Corps (Anzacs) at Gallipoli in 1915. The ensuing battle was a lengthy, deadly stalemate between the Allied forces and the Ottoman army, one that was later employed to represent the 'coming of age' of the newly federated Australia. A century on, the day commemorates the sacrifice of all those in military service.

Regardless of its roots, my memories of Anzac Day are built around food. It is one in a string of days off within the same month – Good Friday, Easter Monday, Labour Day – days filled with barbecues on the deck and stubbies by the pool. With any luck, the weather would be mild, and my sister and I would come home after the dawn service and turn the oven on. On Anzac Day, our love of baking inevitably resulted in Anzac biscuits.

Although the stories that tins of Anzac biscuits were sent to soldiers on the front are a myth, the biscuits played their part in the war. Back home, with poultry farmer ranks depleted, eggs were in short supply. At fetes held to raise money for the war effort, batches of 'soldiers' biscuits' were made with rolled oats, flour, coconut, sugar, butter and golden syrup. The word 'Anzac' is protected in Australia, and can't be used commercially without the permission of the Minister for Veterans' Affairs. They generally turn a blind eye to its use in relation to biscuits – so long as the biscuits in question adhere closely to the original recipe. So, when buying an Anzac, you know what you're getting: a chewy biscuit, filled with oats and coconut, and sweetened with the unmistakable warmth of golden syrup.

I have complicated feelings about Anzac Day. I grew up watching footage of Australians gathered at Gallipoli at dawn, never questioning our 'right' to commemorate in a place where ten times as many Turks died as Anzacs. The concept of the Anzac spirit looms large in my childhood – a lauded masculinity and mateship that reinforce an image of Australia that excludes so many of us. It speaks, too, to the sort of flag-flying patriotism that makes me deeply uncomfortable; the type that seems to want to dwell on what separates rather than unites us.

Despite this, the associations I have with the biscuits themselves are resoundingly positive. Whenever I make them (which is often), I remember my grandma, whose kitchen was never without a well-stocked biscuit jar. I think of those Anzac Day mornings in the car, munching on sweet, chewy biscuits bought in a packet from the supermarket. I reminisce about baking with my sister, sneaking spoonfuls of batter, fingers battling as we fought to clean the bowl. It's impossible to separate them from their origins, but regardless of my feelings on Anzac Day, a century on, the biscuits remain a joy.

ANZAC BISCUITS

Makes 16

125g (4½oz) salted butter
3 tbsp golden syrup
150g (5½oz) plain (all-purpose) flour
100g (3½oz) rolled oats
80g (2¾oz) desiccated coconut
90g (3¼oz) dark brown sugar
60g (2¼oz) caster (superfine) sugar
½ tsp bicarbonate of soda (baking soda)

Preheat the oven to 180°C/350°F/gas mark 4. Melt the butter and golden syrup in a saucepan over a low heat and stir to combine. Put the flour, oats, coconut and sugars into a bowl and mix.

Add the bicarbonate of soda and 1 tablespoon of tap water to the golden syrup and butter, and stir. Pour the liquid over the dry ingredients and mix with a wooden spoon. The mixture should come together in clumps.

Shape the mixture into sixteen balls and place on to baking trays lined with baking paper. Flatten slightly with the back of a spoon. If the biscuits crack at the sides, don't worry, just squidge them back together again – the mixture is incredibly forgiving.

Bake in the oven for 10–12 minutes until golden brown. The biscuits will feel underbaked when you take them out of the oven, but will harden on cooling. Err on the side of slightly underdone: an Anzac biscuit should be chewy.

A Menu for April

by Diana Henry

PORTUGUESE PRAWN PANCAKES

There's nothing people like more than little fried things. I was first cooked these fishy bites by the Portuguese mother of a close friend and I loved them immediately. They're great for dinner parties. Serve them while people are standing around in your kitchen before you sit down to eat.

```
Serves 8 as a starter

120g (4¼oz) plain (all-purpose) flour
150g (5½oz) chickpea flour
1 small onion, very finely chopped
2 garlic cloves, very finely chopped
6 tbsp flat-leaf parsley, finely chopped
450g (1lb) raw prawns (shrimp), chopped
Groundnut (peanut) oil, for frying
Sea salt and lemon wedges, to serve
```

Mix the flours together and, using a small whisk or wooden spoon, gradually add 300ml (10fl oz) of cold water until you have a thick batter. Stir in all the other ingredients. Heat some oil in a frying pan (skillet) over a medium heat and spoon the batter into the pan to make small pancakes, about 4cm (1½in) across. Cook on both sides until golden and the prawns are cooked through. Scatter with salt and serve immediately with wedges of lemon.

ROAST PORK WITH CAPERS, FENNEL AND LEMON

I often serve this at Easter while everyone else is cooking lamb. We really want Easter to be spring-like and sunny but in Britain it can often be cold, even wintry (especially if Easter is early). At such times, pork with a citrusy stuffing is a better option. This is a menu for realists. Serve the pork with cubes of potato roasted with olive oil and thyme or rosemary.

```
Serves 8

1 fennel bulb
1 preserved lemon
1 tbsp olive oil
1 small onion, finely chopped
4 garlic cloves, finely chopped
3 tbsp capers, rinsed
3 tsp honey
Small bunch of flat-leaf parsley, roughly chopped
¼ tsp dried chilli flakes (optional)
2kg (4lb 8oz) belly of pork, boned
300ml (10fl oz) dry white wine
Freshly ground black pepper
```

Halve and quarter the fennel and remove any coarse outer leaves. Trim the tips, cut out the core and discard. Now chop the fennel into little dice. Quarter the preserved lemon, remove and discard the pulp and finely chop the rind.

In a frying pan (skillet), heat the oil and gently cook the onion and fennel until soft, but not coloured. Add the garlic and cook for another couple of minutes, then stir in the capers, preserved lemon rind, honey, chopped parsley, chilli flakes and some pepper (no salt). Leave the stuffing to cool.

Open out the pork and season the inside. Spread the stuffing all over the flesh, then roll up from the long side. Tie tightly at intervals with string.

Preheat the oven to 220°C/425°F/gas mark 7. Put the pork in a roasting tin and rub with olive oil. Season well. Cook for 15 minutes, then turn down the heat to 170°C/340°F/gas mark 3½ and cook for 2 hours. Lift out of the tin on to a warm platter and cover with foil. Leave to rest for 15–20 minutes.

Set the roasting tin over a low heat and add the wine. Scrape to dislodge all the sticky bits then bring to the boil. Keep tasting until it gets to a consistency and flavour you like. Because of the stuffing, the liquid is quite salty, so be careful not to reduce it too much. Serve the pork with cripsy potatoes and offer the hot cooking juices in a jug.

PASTEIS DE NATA

I worked on this recipe for the much-celebrated Portuguese custard tart more than anything I've ever cooked. It's a thrill to pull off your own version.

Makes 28

500g (1lb 2oz) puff pastry
50ml (2fl oz) full-fat milk
2 tbsp cornflour (cornstarch)
250ml (9fl oz) double (heavy) cream
300ml (10fl oz) crème fraîche
135g (5oz) granulated sugar
Pinch of salt
Half a cinnamon stick
Finely grated zest of 1 unwaxed lemon
8 egg yolks
1 tsp vanilla extract

Preheat the oven to 220°C/425°F/gas mark 7. Cut the pastry into quarters and, on a lightly floured surface, roll out each one into a thin rectangle measuring 18 x 25cm (7 x 10in). With the longer side towards you, roll up the pastry to make a log. Trim the ends. Cut each log into seven equal slices.

Take a coil of pastry and press it – putting the pressure on the centre – into the hollow of a round-bottomed bun tin. Keep pressing the pastry to spread it thinly over the base and sides. If it's getting too soft, put the tin in the freezer for a few minutes, then continue. Prick the pastry lightly with a fork. Freeze for 15 minutes, then bake for 5 minutes or until lightly golden. Use a teaspoon to press down the pastry where it has puffed up. Set aside and turn up the heat to 230°C/450°F/gas mark 8.

Mix the milk with the cornflour to form a smooth paste. Put the cream, crème fraîche, sugar, salt, cinnamon and lemon zest in a saucepan. Heat until it comes to just under the boil, stirring to dissolve the sugar. Remove the cinnamon.

In a large bowl, beat the egg yolks, then add the cornflour mixture. Add the warm cream, whisking constantly. Transfer to a clean pan and place on a medium heat. Cook, stirring until the mixture is just under boiling and considerably thickened, but don't let it boil – it should be only a little thicker than double cream. Pour the custard into a jug and stir in the vanilla. Fill the pastry cases with the custard and bake in the oven for 15 minutes, or until the custard is puffed up and blackened in places. Remove from the oven and leave to cool for 10 minutes before carefully running a knife round the edge of the tarts and placing on a wire rack. The filling will deflate but that's normal. Leave for at least 20 minutes before eating.

Reading List

Pat Willard,
Secrets of Saffron
An enticing exploration of the vagabond life of the world's most expensive spice.

Erica Wagner, *Chief Engineer*
An engaging portrait of Washington Roebling, the man who built the Brooklyn Bridge, which will, at any rate, make you glad you were never subjected to any faddish 19th century dietary regimes.

Alana Newhouse,
The 100 Most Jewish Foods
Essays, recipes and stories debating everything from matzo balls to blintzes, with contributions from writers such as Ruth Reichl, Dan Barber and Yotam Ottolenghi.

Elizabeth David,
An Omelette and a Glass of Wine
An eclectic and refreshingly opinionated collection of articles from one of the most revered food writers of all time.

Rachel Khong,
Lucky Peach's All About Eggs
An egg-centric volume from the much-missed cult food magazine exploring everything an egg can be and do.

Kate Young,
The Little Library Year
A thoughtful and beautifully written cookbook that also celebrates the books and characters conjured by each season.

Mem Fox, *Possum Magic*
A classic children's picture book in which the characters set off on a culinary tour of the cities of Australia eating everything from lamingtons to Anzac biscuits.

Diana Henry,
How to Eat a Peach
A fuzzy-covered gem full of menus that take you from an afternoon at the seaside in Brittany to a sultry evening eating mezze in Istanbul.

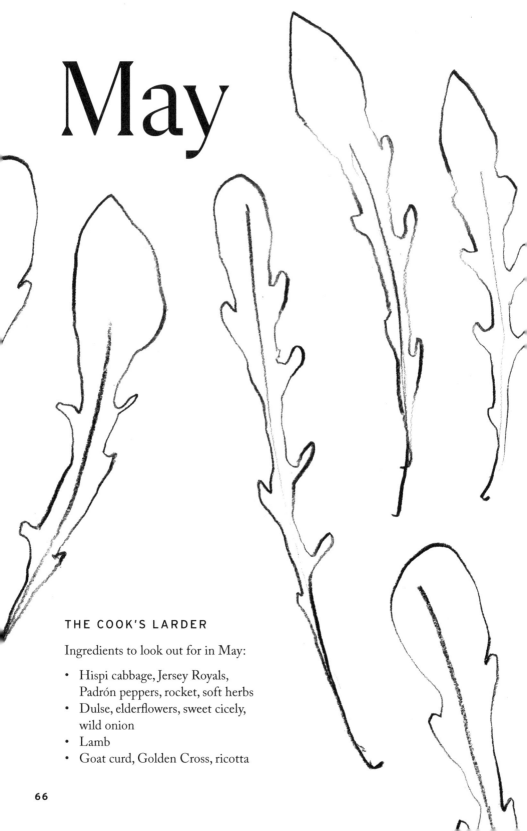

May

THE COOK'S LARDER

Ingredients to look out for in May:

- Hispi cabbage, Jersey Royals, Padrón peppers, rocket, soft herbs
- Dulse, elderflowers, sweet cicely, wild onion
- Lamb
- Goat curd, Golden Cross, ricotta

Everything blooms in May. A lush green rises with the
chaotic dawn chorus and all of nature reacts to the
warming season with a burst of energy and optimism.
It is a time of wild fertility that chimes with ancient
spring festivals around the world; the earliest,
Floralia, celebrating the Roman goddess of flowers with
games and spectacles.

The most languid of foraging trips will yield bagfuls
of cloud-like elderflowers. Bottle their essence in
cordials, vinegars and wines, but save a few to fritter,
then drizzle the golden sprays with orange blossom honey
and eat them while they're hot and crisp.

Despite nature's dramatic growth spurt, we're left
waiting, impatiently, for produce to ripen. Tender leaves
and soft herbs, dressed simply in good oil and lemon
juice, ease the wait. Jersey Royals are plentiful too,
their firm, waxy texture and nutty taste adding structure
to salads — although Margaret Costa believed they
should be served 'absolutely plain in all their pastoral
simplicity — smooth, round, and shiny with butter'.

These promising spring meals, no matter how simple,
are enhanced by small things: flowers, candles, linen
napkins, a jug of water spiked with citrus. And soon
it will be time to fling open the doors and carry these
small things — a procession from kitchen to garden —
to be enjoyed outside.

Edible Flowers

MORE THAN JUST A PRETTY FAD

Edible flowers might seem like the latest food fad, but the art of cooking with flowers has bloomed for many centuries. The ancient Greeks used violet petals in their wine, the Romans were partial to cooking with roses, as were the Ottomans – hence their love of Turkish delight – and the flower-obsessed Victorians sprinkled borage, violets and primroses on salads and cakes.

The lush green of spring is punctuated with colour as plants start to rise and bloom in May, many of which can be picked and enjoyed. Most herb flowers are edible and carry a hazy memory of the plant itself: chive flowers make an excellent vinegar; sage flowers are delicious on pizzas; courgette and pumpkin flowers can be stuffed or pickled; and flavoured butters can be seasoned with the petals of jasmine, orange, lemon or garlic. If there's a glut, flowers can be used to make aromatic drinks: elderflower wine and cordial, anise hyssop syrup and cherry blossom tea.

Picked at dawn before their soft perfume fades in the heat of the sun, rose petals can be made into jellies, jams and sweets, or crystallised along with violets to decorate cakes. In the Middle East, orange blossom water and rose water are important ingredients in countless recipes, from tagines to ma'amoul, the sugar-dusted biscuits filled with dates or nuts that are particularly popular during Easter and Eid.

THE LANGUAGE OF FLOWERS

The Victorians developed a complex form of coded communication through flowers, known as 'floriography' – a way to express feelings in a society obsessed with etiquette. Several floral dictionaries were published, attributing meaning to every pretty petal: mimosa signified chastity, forget-me-nots represented true love and yellow carnations symbolised rejection.

Ma'amoul

by Claudia Roden

These glorious pastries have a melt-in-the-mouth shell and a variety of fillings of dates or nuts – walnuts, pistachios or almonds. My mother always had a biscuit tin full of them to offer with coffee. In Syria and Lebanon they make them with semolina instead of flour.

```
Makes 40

300g (10½oz) soft pitted dates
4–5 tbsp water
500g (1lb 2oz) plain (all-purpose) flour
250g (9oz) unsalted butter, cut into pieces
2–3 tbsp orange blossom or rose water
Up to 4–5 tbsp milk, or as required
Icing (confectioners') sugar, for sprinkling
```

Preheat the oven to 160°C/325°F/gas mark 3.

Cut the dates into pieces. Put them in a saucepan with the water and cook over a low heat, stirring, until they form a soft paste. Set aside to cool.

Put the flour into a bowl and thoroughly work in the butter with your fingers. Add the orange blossom or rose water and the milk – just enough for the dough to hold together – and work until it is soft, malleable and easy to shape.

Take walnut-sized lumps of dough. Roll each one into a ball, make a hole in the centre and enlarge it by pinching the sides up, turning and pressing them against your palm to make a little pot shape. The walls should be quite thin. Any breaks are easily patched. Fill the hole with the date filling to three-quarters full and bring the dough up over the opening to close into a ball. Flatten the filled balls slightly.

Place the pastries on a large baking tray. Make little decorations in the tops of the pastries with tweezers or create little dents with the points of a fork (this will help the sugar to cling after they are baked). Bake for 20–25 minutes. Do not let the pastries become brown or they will be hard and their taste will be spoilt. While they are still warm, they will appear soft and uncooked, but on cooling they will become firm.

When cool, dust the pastries with the sugar. They will keep for a long time in a tightly closed tin.

Salad Days
by Charlotte Mendelson

Adulthood is hard. The news causes palpitations and the small joys that make life worth living – a perfect kiss, a puppy on a trampoline – aren't necessarily there the moment one needs them. A wonderful, soul-enriching lunch, however, is achievable. Necessary, even. And, luckily for us, it doesn't require suckling pig, caviar or ortolans. Not now; not in May. The answer is salad.

I know. But there are salads and salads: a spectrum, at one end of which lies a garnish of wilted lamb's lettuce, a pubic frond of cress, an icy tomato. Move on, past salad bars (sad sweetcorn niblets, bald chickpeas) and supermarket bags (rags of desperate romaine, swampy watercress). Onward, until you reach perfection: a garden salad, grown by you.

I just made one for lunch: it took twenty pleasurable minutes of garden browsing. To a non-cook, this sounds ridiculous. Why not go to the local greasy spoon for a toastie? But if one is food-obsessed, cafés can break your heart; such feeble ingredients, made so little of. Cooking for oneself is a joy and, if one is a gardener-cook, on however modest a scale, there's nothing better than peacefully munching a plateful of leaves and shoots and flowers – the essence of spring.

Today's lunch for one, therefore, consists of a boiled egg and, piled high around it like a jade-and-rainbow cloud: cinnamon and Greek basil; golden marjoram; kale shoots; garlic chives; three kinds of brave bitter chicory; sorrel; chard; wild and tame rocket; Japanese mustards; the sulphur-yellow flowers of neglected brassicas. There is, I notice, technically no lettuce. But there are spicy nasturtium leaves, like lily pads, and their glowing honey-pepper blossoms; tastes of thyme, savory, chervil, shiso, mint, lemon verbena; neon calendula; and borage petals – the hot clear blue of summer skies to come.

That's fine, you may think, for people with rolling acres, orchards, nutteries. I hate them too. My garden consists of wobbling pots on a roof terrace: a scruffy urban jungle, so overstuffed and understyled that guests wince, as if they've witnessed something private. Yes, growing so much in a tiny space is hard work. But it brings joy, peace, flow: one forgets every trouble when faced with a green courgette tendril.

A salad like this is too good for guests. Sprinkle it with oil, salt, lemon; think of it in winter with walnuts, blood orange, feta. It will give you both smug satisfaction and vitamins. It will make you, briefly, happy. Now, that's a lunch.

Fresh Cheese

GREENER PASTURES

Fresh cheeses are at their best in May; the animals are out to pasture, grazing on new grass and producing wonderful milk. Fresh cheeses are the purest expression of the milk's quality and their lightness tends to work well with the more delicately flavoured herbs and vegetables that come into season around this time.

Making fresh cheese at home used to be commonplace. Elizabeth David wrote about how every cookbook, from the 15th to the early 20th century, gave recipes for fresh milk cheeses, which were either eaten the day they were made, with cream and sugar, or salted and stored in stoneware jars.

If you haven't made your own fresh cheese before, start with something simple: tip a pot of yogurt into a muslin, hang it over a bowl and leave it overnight. The resulting cream cheese, or labneh, is delicious with both sweet and savoury flavours. Drizzle it with olive oil, salt and za'atar to make a dip, or serve with honey, nuts and fruit. Graduate to something a little more complex by heating milk with lemon juice (or rennet, if you can find it), or simply find a good cheesemonger and pick the freshest cheeses throughout spring – from ricotta and curd to goat's cheeses moulded into logs and pyramids.

Bolters

by Catherine Phipps

Years ago I was in a tiny mountain village in the Mani region of the Greek Peloponnese. I was there for the taverna's infamous lamb chops, but instead I found myself bowled over by the side dishes: the *horta*, Greece's ubiquitous wild greens; the warm beetroots served with their own leaves; and best of all, the *gigantes*.

The flavour of the beans was elusive: close to tarragon or maybe chervil, but with more depth, less aniseed. I argued with my mother about what the herb might be. As a local, she was adamant it wouldn't be tarragon. Eventually, the cook produced a bundle of flat-leaf parsley, but it was parsley that had bolted. The plump, serrated leaves had elongated into fronds and the flavour was quite different – less grassy and astringent, instead softer and subtle. Was this really what had transformed the flavour of the beans? It was.

It was the first time I had truly appreciated how the flavour and aroma of a plant could change so dramatically over a growing season and I have paid attention to this ever since. My herb patch is testament to the phenomenon. Every spring I wait for the overwintered parsley to reach for the sun, knowing it will stretch and mellow into a flavour I love. I cut it back and freeze it, bundling stems together for stock and reserving the fronds for my own pots of beans.

Another good 'bolter' is coriander. This is serendipitous as I am useless at producing lush, bushy plants. Here, the flavour becomes sweeter, with a hint of cinnamon, less citrus. I harvest, then finely chop the stems to freeze and shake into all kinds of things, while the delicate leaves are used immediately and sparingly.

I always want more than I can produce but, happily, grocers that sell generous unwrapped bunches of herbs will often have thick-stemmed parsley and coriander that were clearly racing to set seed. I treasure these when I find them. In a world of culinary conformity, it is wonderful to be able to appreciate even the minutest of seasonal variations.

POTHERBS

The modern gardener and cook has, by historical standards, a narrow view of what a herb might be. In the monastic or castle garden, every plant that was not listed as a fruit tree was a herb. In fact, all vegetables that grew above the ground were called herbs or potherbs until around the 18th century.

Mezzaluna

Mezzaluna, meaning 'half moon', is the Italian name for a semi-circular knife designed to be held with two hands. The name, referencing the curved shape of the blade, hints at the romance of a tool that has largely disappeared from our kitchen drawers. Yet there is proper efficiency behind the romantic name: the blade's rhythmic rocking motion is perfectly suited to chopping fresh green herbs until they are fine but not pulp; and the double handle means fingers remain intact, however fast you chop. Ingredients that might be pulverised by a food processor can be thrown into the mix as well. Add lemon peel and garlic to chopped parsley to make gremolata, or combine herbs and spices such as parsley, oregano, garlic and chilli for chimichurri. Large mezzalunas can also be used to mince meat – they will produce a better steak tartare or burger than any other kitchen tool – and will neatly slice pizza without disturbing the molten cheese.

A Menu for May
by Olia Hercules

SPRING BROTH WITH BUCKWHEAT DUMPLINGS AND SORREL

Herb stalks have a lot of wonderful flavour locked inside them, so don't rush to chuck them in the bin. Collect a whole bunch, bruise them lightly and use as a bouquet garni of sorts. Added to a vegetable or meat stock at the end of cooking, it gives a subtle aromatic layer to a broth. Watercress or nettles can be added along with the sorrel used here, or served as a good substitute.

```
Serves 4-6

2 tbsp sunflower oil
1 onion, diced
1 large carrot, diced
1 leek, white part only, diced
4 garlic cloves, chopped
1.5 litres (2¾ pints) cold water
300g (10½oz) fresh aromatic herb stalks, such as tarragon,
coriander (cilantro), basil, dill
50g (1¾oz) sorrel (and/or watercress, blanched nettles)
Sea salt

For the dumplings:
1 large egg
3 tbsp kefir or plain yogurt
½ tsp fine sea salt
120g (4¼oz) buckwheat flour
Small handful of soft herbs (same as above or whatever you have),
finely chopped
```

Heat the oil in a heavy-based pan over a low heat, then add the onion. Let it soften and get some colour, then add the carrot and leek and cook them over a medium heat, stirring from time to time – you are aiming to get them nicely caramelised. Sorrel is sour so we want to inject lots of sweetness into the liquor. Lastly, add the garlic and cook for a couple of minutes until golden. Pour in the cold water and season the stock well with sea salt.

Bring the water to a simmer, lower the heat and add the gently bruised stalks. You will take them out soon – they are there simply to infuse and add flavour. Tying them like a bouquet garni will make the job easier.

To make the dumplings, whisk the egg, kefir and sea salt together and add the flour. Mix in the chopped herbs. The mix should have the consistency of a thick cake batter.

Fish out the herb stalks from the broth and discard. Increase the heat slightly. Scoop up teaspoonfuls of the batter and drop them into the broth to form dumplings. Cook for about 5 minutes.

To serve, place the chopped sorrel into each serving bowl and pour over the herb broth and dumplings.

LAMB COOKED IN HERBS AND TAMARIND

This recipe is inspired by a Georgian dish called *chakapuli*. Lamb is slow-cooked in a pot with a little water, verjuice, tarragon and whole sour plums, until tender. For this recipe, you can use any number of soft herbs. You can also replace the tamarind with 3–4 preserved lemons or sour plums – just blitz them into a purée and add with the herbs and spices.

```
Serves 6-8

75g (2½oz) fresh coriander (cilantro), leaves and stalks, chopped
50g (1¾oz) fresh dill, leaves and stalks, chopped
50g (1¾oz) fresh tarragon, leaves only
50g (1¾oz) fresh mint, leaves only
4 spring onions (scallions), roughly chopped
2 tbsp honey
4 garlic cloves, chopped
2 tbsp coriander seeds, lightly toasted and crushed
1 tbsp fennel seeds, lightly toasted and crushed
2 tbsp sunflower oil
100g (3½oz) tamarind paste
1 lamb shoulder or leg
Sea salt
```

Preheat the oven to 180°C/350°F/gas mark 4. In a food processor, blitz half of the herbs, and all of the spring onions, honey, garlic and spices with the oil and the tamarind paste. Add the salt to taste – it should be well-seasoned, herby and slightly sweet-and-sour. Rub the paste all over the lamb and wrap it in foil.

Place the lamb on a baking tray and cook for 30 minutes, then lower the heat to 160°C/320°F/gas mark 3 and cook for around 2–3 hours, until the meat is tender and falls off the bone.

Serve with new potatoes, tossed in some of the herby lamb juices. Pour the rest of the juices over the lamb like gravy and sprinkle with the remaining herbs.

RICOTTA AND HONEY CHEESECAKE

In Poland and Ukraine, where I was raised, we use fresh curd cheese called *twaróg* to make a simple but delicious baked cheesecake. Semolina is often used, but I find that polenta adds a nice texture. If you can find or make twaróg, do use it. Otherwise a good-quality ricotta or cottage cheese will work really well. Serve with a seasonal fruit compote.

150g (5½oz) unsalted butter, softened, plus extra for greasing
100g (3½oz) runny honey
100g (3½oz) coconut sugar
3 eggs, separated
1 tsp vanilla extract
500g (1lb 2oz) ricotta or cottage cheese
120g (4oz) fine polenta (cornmeal)
Pinch of salt

Preheat the oven to 180°C/350°F/gas mark 4 and grease a 20cm (8in) cake tin with butter.

Put the softened butter into the bowl of an electric mixer fitted with the whisk attachment, along with the honey and 80g (2¾oz) of the coconut sugar. Whisk until fluffy and light.

Beat the egg yolks with a fork and gradually add them, whisking well, then whisk in the vanilla extract and cheese. Fold in the polenta. Leave for at least 10 minutes, so the polenta has time to absorb the moisture and soften.

Whisk the egg whites until they start frothing up. Add the remaining 20g (¾oz) of coconut sugar and the salt and keep whisking until you have soft peaks. Now take a large spoonful of the egg-white mixture and fold it quite vigorously into the cheese mixture to loosen it up. Add the rest of the egg-white mixture in three batches, folding it in gently but with confidence, making sure it is thoroughly incorporated. Using a silicone spatula, gently scrape the mixture into the cake tin and bake for 40 minutes, or until it is a little wobbly, but not liquid. Leave the cheesecake in its tin to rest and cool, then slice and serve.

Reading List

Frances Bissell,
The Scented Kitchen
Inventive floral recipes that encourage the cook to move beyond mixing a few nasturtium petals into a salad. Try the frozen elderflower margaritas.

Claudia Roden,
A Book of Middle Eastern Food
The seminal book on Middle Eastern cooking, originally published in 1968, which mixes evocative stories with meticulously researched recipes. Credited with introducing cooks around the world to za'atar, tahini and preserved lemons.

Charlotte Mendelson,
Rhapsody in Green
A humorous memoir from a novelist who transformed her tiny urban patio into a garden larder.

Marta McDowell,
Emily Dickinson's Gardening Life
The plants and places that inspired the iconic American poet.

Claudia Lucero, *One-Hour Cheese*
A beginner's guide to making fresh cheese at home, from paneer to ricotta to mozzarella.

Catherine Phipps, *Leaf*
An innovative cookbook celebrating edible leaves in all their versatility.

Bee Wilson,
Consider the Fork
The unsung history of our kitchens and the everyday objects we take for granted.

Olia Hercules, *Mamushka*
A personal collection of recipes that illustrates the culinary depth of Ukraine and Eastern Europe. The recipe for *pampushka* (Ukrainian garlic bread) is a must.

June

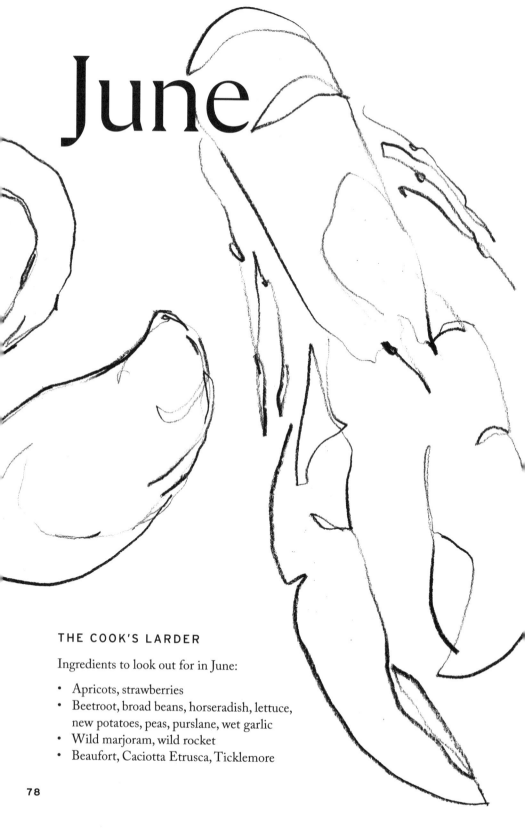

THE COOK'S LARDER

Ingredients to look out for in June:

- Apricots, strawberries
- Beetroot, broad beans, horseradish, lettuce, new potatoes, peas, purslane, wet garlic
- Wild marjoram, wild rocket
- Beaufort, Caciotta Etrusca, Ticklemore

As the days lengthen, there's time to linger over meals.
Venture outdoors – short sleeves, bare skin – and bask
in the warmth of early summer. Impromptu grazing comes
into its own: sitting on a stone wall overlooking a small
harbour and sucking the shells of sweet shellfish bought
from a nearby shack; park gatherings with nothing but
a bottle of wine and salty snacks, greasy fingertips
pressing into paper cups; dragging a mismatch of tables
and chairs under dappled shade and feasting until you
reach a 'happy state of haziness', as Nancy Mitford once
described it.

Everything is fresh and new and green: wet garlic,
delicate and sweet, broad beans and peas eaten straight
from the pod – a simple tactile pleasure. The change in
light and temperature is felt at sea too: lobsters and
crabs are stirring and mackerel are plentiful, moving
inshore as the water warms.

At last there is fruit – strawberries and apricots –
the sweet scents of early summer. Strawberries are best
enjoyed straight from the punnet, only improved by a
tumble with lemon and icing sugar if they've been picked
too soon. If there's a glut, make jam. M.F.K. Fisher,
reminiscing about making strawberry and apricot jams as a
child, recalls how 'the hot kitchen sent out tantalising
clouds, and the fruit on the porch lay rotting in its
crates, or readied for the pots and the wooden spoons, in
fair glowing piles upon the juice-stained tables'. These
glowing piles are only the beginning; soon there will be
more glorious gluts to gorge on.

Broad Beans

THE PLEASURE OF PODDING

There's something wonderfully therapeutic about podding broad beans (fava beans). Running a thumb down the thick seam, flicking each bean from its downy bed, one by one, until there is a satisfying heap and a tangle of debris. Unless the beans are particularly young, it's best to double-pod: the tough outer skin crinkles when blanched and comes away with a nick and a squeeze. It's worth it just to reveal the vibrant green colour.

Pretty white and purple flowers spread over the fields in spring – sweet-smelling and promising good things – and the beans are ready to pick in early summer. Whether in the field or at the market, choose the smaller pods for the most tender beans, then look to British and Italian recipes to inspire you.

WHAT TO DO WITH BROAD BEANS

- Eat straight from the pod with young, hard sheep's cheese (see Rachel Roddy's menu at the end of the chapter).
- Spoon olive oil-drenched beans over bruschetta spread with ricotta.
- Purée and serve with fish or lamb, or turn into a dip.
- Add to spring broths, stews and risottos.
- Cook with bacon or pancetta and serve with thick slices of crusty bread.
- Mash with anchovies, chilli, lemon zest and glugs of olive oil, then spoon over burrata.
- Toss with asparagus tips, fresh herbs, lemon and olive oil for a simple salad.
- Pound in a pestle and mortar and garnish with gremolata.
- Stuff into cooked artichokes with a little cream and a squeeze of lemon.
- Save the pods if they're in good shape and make them into a purée or soup.

King of Fruits
by Helena Lee

There were several things that separated me from a normal suburban British existence. One of those was the durian. Our family did not keep skeletons, but durians in the closet (the airing cupboard, to be exact); somewhere warm to ripen the fruit, where it sat perfuming our towels with its particular fragrance – a heady mix of putrid sweetness and gas.

When your mother is from Malaysia, as mine is, you have to learn to accept the peculiarities of the durian's appeal, to understand its cult-like following. For this unwieldy beast has no place in the fruit bowl next to the refined elegance of a peach or the Mediterranean assurance of a lemon. One might assume that the 'King of Fruits', as it is known in Southeast Asia where it grows and flourishes, is universally adored, but this could not be further from the truth. The durian is divisive as a despot – worshipped by some and reviled by others. But none can escape the tyrannical clutches of its aroma once unleashed. So pungent is its perfume that the fruit is banned on certain airlines and public transport networks. In fact, one audacious aunt went to great lengths to smuggle pieces from Malaysia to England in glass jars sealed with wax, suffocated in ziplock bags and buried deep in her luggage in the hold. The durian really is forbidden fruit.

Once ripe, the ritual of unpeeling would begin. There's jeopardy inherent in its architecture, so this was no easy task. The size of a human head, the durian resembles a weapon of war with its mace-like spikes – a deterrent for the novice or the foolhardy. My mother was deft in identifying the fault lines, defining them with a cleaver, then using the weight of her body, and the thorns, as leverage to prise open the outer casing with the palms of her hands. It sometimes took three heaves before the tough rind would finally crack open, rewarding perseverance with such treasure inside: nestling in each segment would be perfectly plump pale-yellow pillows. Plucked from their beds, each piece was generous in flavour with a scent that was both fetid and alluring, perhaps of bananas on the cusp of fermentation, perhaps of overly sweet caramel. The flesh, as creamy and unsubtle as egg custard, would yield easily, and we would eat greedily, mercilessly, illicitly. This annual event became the knowledge that was passed on from mother to daughter – my cultural rite of passage.

Gawai
by Anna Sulan Masing

Gawai celebrates the end of harvest and the beginning of the new farming cycle for indigenous peoples in Borneo. In Sarawak it is officially marked on 1 June, when most travel back to their family villages to celebrate, bearing gifts. Within the Iban community, the largest indigenous group, traditions vary depending on migration histories. Upriver in the Baleh region the rituals are rooted in war due to the dangers of travelling deep into the interior. Their bards tell stories inviting Lang, the god of war, to the table. Across all homes in Sarawak at Gawai, food, *tuak* (homemade rice wine), music, dancing and stories fill the air.

The Iban diaspora continue Gawai festivities – remembering home and celebrating with friends and families in their new places of belonging; creating new rituals and stories. Like harvest festivals the world over, it is about coming together and the beginning of something new.

Aya Lang nadai aku nentang pandok ranggang mau gemurong
Ayay Lang Jugu nadai aku ditu ditu enggau anggu ketapu gantong
Menuang abi di dabang, lensi betundai tinggi:
Kitai bala pengabang sapa pandai ngambi?

Nowhere can I see Lang, our fiery god of war,
Nowhere among us can be seen his headdress so resplendent
As one who notches and fells a tree:
Who then among us will tell the gods of our wish that
they should join us?

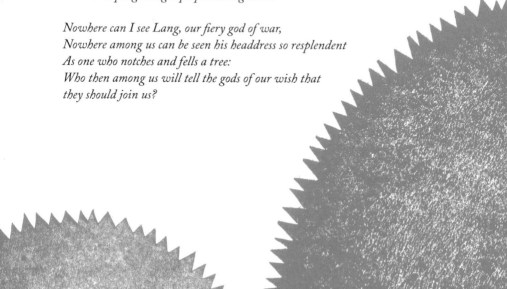

The Party

Sun prickles her forearm,
The beginning of heat, the promise of warmth,
Stretching out both arms she wiggles her fingers, and closes her eyes.
The hour before the party,
Almost ready, the first of the season's fruit on the table to cut;
strawberries, before they know that sweetness of an almost rot
The moment of anticipation, waiting,
The hour before the party —
June.

The doorbell rings.
She starts. She's not ready.

'Sorry I'm early,' he says.
She smiles. He thrusts the fruit to her.
It prickles her inner arms.
Her head bends to it, breathing in the pungent smell and she
thinks of home.
She grips it close to her chest, spikes digging into her —
Durian.

She adjusts her sarong.
Woven by her great-grandmother. From a time that's past.

Later, drunk on Riesling, doused in the smoke of the barbecue,
She takes the biggest knife she has, to the King of Fruits.
Beneath the husk, the fleshy stones sit,
Her friend Safiah laughs at the reactions of the uninitiated —
'Aye ya, hopefully one day you will understand this gift.'

She is passed a glass of tuak.
'Sungai aku, bejalai aku' she can hear her grandmother say.
My river, my journey.

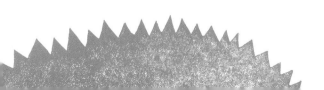

Unhampered Pleasures
by Felicity Cloake

I'll let you into a secret. Every summer I'm asked to write about the perfect picnic, regular as clockwork, and most of the time I do it, even though I know full well those winsome wicker baskets and Kilner jars are more pleasurable on the page than in real life. That fancy hamper is a bastard to carry; the rug will immediately be carpeted with plastic packaging, and somehow I always forget the corkscrew. Perfection, it seems, is a dish best enjoyed in the sunlit uplands of the imagination.

The most memorable picnics are less carefully curated. I don't know why the cheese and pickle sandwich purchased at a service station on the M54 and eaten in the rain at the top of a Snowdonian peak sticks in the mind years later, but it does. And I maintain that no fruit cake has ever tasted as good as the leftover hunk shared out as a peace offering in an Alpine meadow in midsummer, shortly after it became apparent that I'd left our cheese and ham baguettes in the hotel lobby several hours and many miles previously.

The path of my life is scattered with squashed quiches and warm Oranginas, sausage rolls and sugary cans of Irn-Bru, consumed at the side of minor roads to a soundtrack of amiable honks from passing agricultural vehicles. Riding around France a couple of years ago we pedalled for four hours through Alsace-Lorraine without passing a single shop. After 55 kilometres in the saddle, we stopped by

a perfectly picturesque babbling brook for a stale madeleine apiece, half a chalky bar of rain-damaged chocolate and a hearty swig of local eau de vie. They went down a treat.

It's as much to do with the anticipation as the meal itself – the prospect of a picnic is a glad one whether you're puffing up a mountain on two wheels or speeding down it on two planks of fibreglass, and by the time you actually stop, whatever it is has taken on the savour of the finest of feasts. The Tuscan hills look even more beautiful with an increasingly greasy bag of focaccia hovering on the horizon, and the warm weight of a black-pudding roll in your jersey pocket in the Hebrides feels something like heaven, while no so-called sports drink could hope to refresh like half a dozen oysters arranged on a Breton sea wall like so many saline shots.

Gourmet or not, when you feel you've earned your lunch, there's a basic satisfaction in being hungry enough to plonk yourself down anywhere (generally on a thistle or a cowpat, if you're me) and cram it into your mouth with nary a bamboo beaker or gingham napkin in sight. From a Provençal *pan bagnat* to a packet of out-of-date crisps, it's funny how almost anything tastes great at the top of a big hill.

Blue Sky Drinking
by Aimee Hartley

It's a curious thing, wine. Noble in nature, it sits at the table with an air of formality. Sometimes the bottle is placed out of arm's reach, for it has fallen to another soul to fill our glasses as they empty. But nowhere is there a greater sense of freedom when drinking wine than outdoors. The rules are undone. Gone are the formalities of service and the elaborate glassware: paper cups reign. Bottles sit where they are told, wonky on picnic blankets or wedged into the ground. Styles are chosen not with a particular meal in mind, but according to how well they drink under blue skies.

There are some important things to remember when drinking outdoors:

- Do not forget your corkscrew. Your trusty waiter's friend should remain in your bag all summer long, equipped to deal with impromptu wine openings whenever the mood takes.
- Paper cups are preferable to plastic, unless you can find yourself the king of all reusable glasses, Govino.
- Never has the wine sleeve had such an important role – keep one (preferably two) in the freezer, ready to slip onto your wine of choice to keep it perfectly chilled beneath the sun.

The palest form of Provençal rosé often takes the crown in summer. But look beyond pretty pinks; good rosé is not simply about colour, nor is it a style of wine to be overlooked. Like biting into a perfectly ripe peach, it should be gloriously refreshing but have a little personality, too. The Portuguese know this well, and *palhete* – a style of wine that blends white and red grapes together – gives you the best of both worlds.

Red wine often gets shunned in the height of summer, but light, joyous reds – coined by the French as *vin de soif* – served chilled, are your new best friend. Look to the Gamay grape in Beaujolais and Cabernet Franc in the Loire for sure-fire fun and drinkability.

Fizz needn't be on procession, and should be opened whenever the heart desires. For an adventure, seek out a style known as *pétillant naturel* (or 'Pét-Nat' for short) – the wilder, more naturally minded sibling to Champagne. Several scoops of ice cream wouldn't go amiss at this point. Sip from your paper cup as the sun begins to lower, and let the wine flow as effortlessly as the long summer days.

A Menu for June

by Rachel Roddy

FRESH BROAD BEANS AND PECORINO CHEESE

Eating raw broad beans straight from their pods with young Pecorino Romano cheese is a Roman spring ritual that everyone partakes in, especially at picnics. The combination of bright green beans – small, tender, sweet and tasting like pure chlorophyll – contrasting with the sharp, creamy cheese is a triumph. It is a ritual full of symbolism for Romans who consider *fava* beans harbingers of spring – a custom that reminds us that it isn't just what you eat, but how.

Put a pile of beans, a hunk of Pecorino and a stumpy knife in the middle of the table and leave everyone to get on with it.

IMPANATA

Every town in Sicily has its own version of *impanata*, which means 'in bread'; it is a bread dough pie filled with whatever is abundant. The most common filling in the town of Gela, our summer home, is wild greens and anchovies. My favourite, though, is mozzarella and anchovies, which makes for a soft and deeply savoury filling that stretches like a telephone cord when hot. It is a delicious and portable thing.

```
Serves 4-6

7g (¼oz) dried yeast or 15g (½oz) fresh yeast
1 tbsp caster (superfine) sugar
400g (14oz) '00' flour
10g (¼oz) salt
2 tablespoons extra virgin olive oil

For the filling:
500g (1lb 2oz) mozzarella, well-drained and torn
10 anchovy fillets
A little olive oil mixed with water, or 1 beaten egg
Salt and freshly ground black pepper
```

In a small bowl, dissolve the yeast and sugar in 50ml (2fl oz) warm water until it froths.

In a large bowl, mix the flour, salt and olive oil, then add the dissolved yeast and 250ml (9fl oz) water to bring everything together into a soft dough. With oiled hands, knead and fold the dough into a smooth ball. Transfer to a lightly oiled bowl, cover with a cloth or cling film, then leave in a warm spot for 2 hours, or until doubled in size.

Preheat the oven to 200°C/400°F/gas mark 6.

Lightly oil a 28cm (11in) diameter baking tin. Cut the dough in half and roll it out into circles – one should be larger than the tin, the other the size of the tin. Press the big piece into the tin, making sure it comes up the sides. Rub the dough with a little olive oil. Arrange the cheese and anchovies evenly on the dough and sprinkle with a little salt and pepper. Brush the edges with oil, then cover with the remaining dough. Pinch and twist the edges closed. Brush with either oil mixed with water or beaten egg.

Make a slit in the top with a knife and bake for 25–35 minutes, or until golden and puffed up.

SUMMER TART

A summer tart taught to me by the Roman pastry chef Sara Levi. The pastry is what is often known as rough puff, and is very forgiving, as is the filling – pick the ripest fruit you can find.

Makes 1 large tart measuring approximately 25–30cm (10–12in)

250g (9oz) '00' flour
1–2 tbsp caster (superfine) sugar
Pinch of salt
175g (6oz) cold unsalted butter, plus 2–3 thin slices
90ml (3fl oz) iced water
5–8 firm but ripe plums, apricots or peaches, cut into wedges
80g (2¾oz) demerara (raw brown) sugar
1 egg, beaten, for the egg wash

Sift the flour, caster sugar and salt into a large bowl. Dice the cold butter into 3cm (1¼in) pieces. Using your fingertips, quickly rub the butter into the flour leaving some chunks of butter in the mix to help with flakiness. Add the iced water and pull the pastry together with a spatula so as not to work it too much. Gather it into a ball, cover with baking paper and rest in the fridge for at least 2 hours.

Preheat the oven to 180°C/350°F/gas mark 4 and line a shallow baking tray with baking paper.

On a floured work surface, roll out the pastry to a thickness of about ½ cm (¼in) and lay over the prepared baking tray. Line with wedges of seasonal fruit and sprinkle with some of the demerara sugar and a couple of slices of butter. Fold the edges of the pastry over the fruit, paint with an egg wash and sprinkle the pastry lip with a little more sugar.

Bake for about 40 minutes, until fully golden – resist the urge to take it out earlier as the bottom needs time to cook.

Reading List

Ping Coombes, *Malaysia*
There are far too few books on
Malaysian food. This *MasterChef*
winner brings it into the spotlight,
drawing inspiration from her mother's
recipes and the street markets in her
hometown of Ipoh.

Margaret Brooke,
My Life in Sarawak
The adventures of Margaret de Windt,
who married the Rajah of Sarawak in
1869, offering a rare glimpse of life in
colonial Borneo.

Felicity Cloake,
One More Croissant for the Road
A two-wheeled 2,350km Tour de
France in search of the best recipes
for Gallic classics, from tarte tatin
to cassoulet.

Kermit Lynch,
Adventures on the Wine Route
A chronicle of Lynch's peregrinations
through rural France, packed with
vivid anecdotes and tart observations.

Salvador Dalí,
The Wines of Gala
An eccentric guide that explores the
many myths of the grape, alongside
sensuous and subversive works by the
artist, always true to his maxim that 'a
real connoisseur does not drink wine
but tastes of its secrets'.

M.F.K. Fisher, *Musings on Wine
and Other Libations*
An anthology of the finest writing on
wine from one of the greatest food
writers of the 20th century.

Rachel Roddy, *Two Kitchens*
Family recipes from Rome and Sicily,
peppered with personal stories. Try the
panelle di Fabrizia (Fabrizia's chickpea
fritters) with a cold beer.

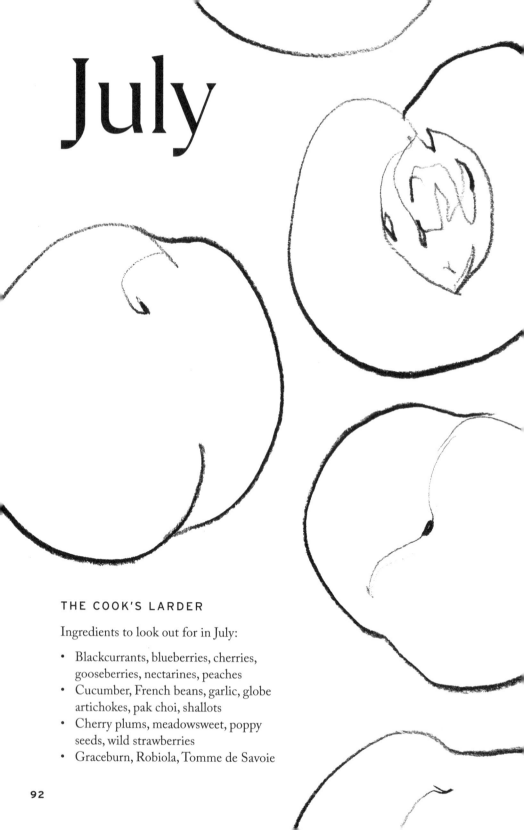

July

THE COOK'S LARDER

Ingredients to look out for in July:

- Blackcurrants, blueberries, cherries, gooseberries, nectarines, peaches
- Cucumber, French beans, garlic, globe artichokes, pak choi, shallots
- Cherry plums, meadowsweet, poppy seeds, wild strawberries
- Graceburn, Robiola, Tomme de Savoie

'Summer afternoon; to me those have always been the two most beautiful words in the English language,' wrote Henry James. Indeed, those words evoke a dreamy languor: sitting under a tree with a good book, a nonchalant hand dipping into a bag of crisps, a long, cool drink refreshing the palate after each salty bite. Perhaps, also, a bowl of unadorned cherries, ripe peaches with their almost indecent musk, a half-finished, hastily prepared sandwich.

Appetite can be fickle in the heat. Forays into the kitchen are brief: there's no need for culinary ingenuity when fresh produce is bountiful and at its best. It's more a matter of assembling than cooking, with a quick improvised dressing the only exertion required. 'How one learns to dread the season for salads in England,' lamented Elizabeth David in 1955. 'An abused, neglected thing,' chimed Laurie Colwin, cooking in her tiny New York apartment in the 1980s. How times have changed. Today, lettuces with romantic names can be bought with ease — batavia, romaine, oak leaf, lollo rosso — and dressed with a dizzying choice of oils, citrus and vinegars. Choose the freshest leaves, dress them gently with your hands, taste as you go and season well — the salad can be redeemed.

Finish each meal with whatever fruit is in season: blueberries, cherries, melons, nectarines and peaches. 'All cooked food aspires to the condition of fruit,' states Harold McGee. In other words, fruit is perfect just the way it is. But if you desire spectacle, look to the 'macédoine of fruit' or 'le grand dessert' that glorified the sumptuous tables of the 19th century: elaborate platters of fruits and ices served with delicate biscuits or almond tuiles. Beats canned fruit cocktail any day.

Gooseberries

A CELEBRATION OF SOUR

Eat a raw gooseberry early in the season and your face will pucker like a baby eating lemons. Firm and sharp in May and June, when it's best to cook the berries with a little sugar, they sweeten just a month later and can be eaten straight from the punnet.

Gooseberries perform their spritely dance particularly well in puddings. Whip them into syllabubs – described as 'the party pudding of the English' by Elizabeth David – add to Eton Mess and summer puddings, or make dessert for breakfast with a simple gooseberry and oat cake. Making a classic gooseberry fool – a 'delightful nonsensical bit of folly', according to Jane Grigson, and the 'kind of thing that women are said to favour, but men eat more of' – is perhaps the best thing you can do with the fruit.

Embrace the sourness, use a little less sugar in your recipes, and allow the glorious sharp flavour to reign. Making a simple purée is the easiest and most versatile way to start. Tip the gooseberries into a pan with just enough water to cover the base. Cook slowly over a gentle heat until the berries have collapsed. Press through a sieve – add sugar to suit and freeze what you don't need – and you'll have the perfect base for compote, ice cream and cocktails.

Of course, sourness needn't be tempered, and the zing of gooseberries can be used in savoury dishes, too. Make a sauce or relish to serve with mackerel – such a perfect pairing that the French call the gooseberry *groseille à maquereau*, 'the mackerel currant' – although it's also good with goose, duck and pork. Push the berries into focaccia dough before it bakes, or soup up the sourness by pickling them to make a Japanese-style *umeboshi*.

BERRY BLENDS

Jostaberries are a cross between a gooseberry and blackcurrant and taste equally of the two. Look out for other delicious horticultural experiments, such as tayberries and boysenberries, throughout the summer months.

Sour
by Mark Diacono

When I first made sherbet lemons, the perfume of calamine lotion filled my nose – not from the cooking process, but from that curious part of the brain that so vividly recreates the memory of a familiar scent. This strange synaptic connection owes everything to the first time I got seriously sunburnt. I'd been sitting on the beach worrying a sherbet Dip Dab and a bag of sherbet lemons that was becoming ever stickier in the sun, immune to the punishment my pasty ten-year-old hide was taking. I finished the sherbet lemons that evening, face down on the floor, my mum swirling the supposedly relieving lotion over my radiating shoulders.

My enjoyment of sour was at its natural height then, in the years before I ran off like a middle-aged Ferrari driver into an ill-advised affair with too much sugar. I've fallen heavily back in love with sourness over the last decade, and at no time am I more besotted than in high summer.

The frostbitten labels in the freezer tell me I spent my birthday last July bagging an entire drawerful of green and purple gooseberries, while jars in the cupboard read 'Gooseberry Curd', 'Gooseberry Umeboshi' and 'Gooseberry Vinegar'; all capturing one of my favourite sours for cold weather pleasure. The phone pics I take as recipe reminders are full of lively sharp salsas, rojaks dusted with chaat masala or dotted with passion fruit; there are pomegranates in all forms – powder, juice, molasses and seed – on everything from ice cream to curries; and citrus spikes every drink, from homemade lemonade to the Tom Collins that leaves me capable of anything after one and incapable of anything after two.

While salt, sweet, bitter and umami all offer pleasure, nothing thrills like sour. That sensation – whether eye-popping, eye-closing or a more subtle punctuation – has become an essential part of summer to me. And whether it's the 'chicken' of their sourness, or the 'egg' of my calamine-sun association, I now make sherbet lemons every July.

Cichèti and Bitters

by Russell Norman

The Venetian tradition of serving small glasses of wine with small snacks (*ombre* and *cichèti* in local dialect) goes back many centuries. Casanova was known to partake enthusiastically at the cosy Do Spade, a wine bar that's still going today, tucked away down a tiny alleyway near the Rialto Bridge. It's difficult to know whether the booze was meant to supplement the food or vice versa, but the custom persists and these days some of the best food in the city is served in those little bars the locals call *bàcari*. The best are concentrated around Rialto Market and the philosophy of serving 'market-to-table' dishes is practised quite literally on an hourly basis. Francesco Pinto at the excellent All'Arco, for example, walks between the market stalls and his tiny wine bar several times a day with armfuls of fresh fish, live crustacea, vegetables, cured hams and cheese.

But modern tastes have evolved somewhat and you are just as likely to see delicious morsels of authentic, seasonal food served with an array of bitters and spritzes. Campari, Aperol, Select and Cynar are the most common aperitivo ingredients, the familiar red glow of the first coming from crushed cochineal beetles, and the wonderful bitter profile of the last from artichokes.

Matching cichèti to aperitivi is always going to be hit-and-miss, because the nature of cichèti means that you will eat several snacks with a variety of flavours in a typical half-hour session. But after many years of research and practice, here are my tips for that perfect combination of bitter and sweet – the tantalising taste Italians call *agrodolce*.

VOWEL LANGUAGE

Venetian dialect has an aversion to consonants. Sometimes it disposes of them altogether. The Italian word for flavour, *sapore*, becomes *saor* in Venice, and soft-shell crabs, *moleche*, are always referred to as *moeche*. But mostly it's simply double consonants that offend, so whereas in standard Italian the spelling is *cicchetti*, in Venetian it's always *cichèti*.

CAMPARI

The relatively high alcohol content and intense bitterness of Campari suit it perfectly to subtle dilution with sympathetic ingredients. With soda and a slice of orange, or with vermouth in an Americano, it goes well with fatty snacks such as *sopressa* and *cotechino* (both deliciously soft sausages). The best iteration and match, in my opinion, is to make a Negroni (equal parts gin, Campari and sweet vermouth over ice) and enjoy it with Cantabrian anchovies on thinly sliced cold butter placed on cold toasted sourdough.

APEROL

Sweeter and lower in alcohol content than Campari, Aperol is best used in a Venetian spritz. But unlike the rest of the world, bars in Venice prefer a local still white wine (such as Soave) and extremely fizzy seltz to make their spritz, rather than Prosecco. An Aperol spritz goes wonderfully well with gently fried and pickled sardines, melted onions, raisins and pine nuts – the classic Venetian speciality known as *sarde in saor.*

SELECT

The only bitter aperitivo made in Venice, originally produced in a warehouse near the Arsenale in the Castello district, Select has a viscosity that tends to complement hot flavours very well. Serve it half-and-half with white wine over ice and a slice of lemon to make a Bicicletta, and try it with a small spicy sandwich made with 'nduja and plenty of Tabasco.

CYNAR

The island of Sant'Erasmo in the Venetian lagoon is world-famous for its purple artichokes and this miraculous liqueur manages to convey the unique bitter flavour in liquid form. It's wonderful when mixed in equal parts with a gentle bottle-fermented Prosecco, a few ice cubes and a slice of lemon, and it is the perfect accompaniment to *baccalà mantecato*, the delightfully light and fluffy creamed salt cod, emulsified with olive oil and a little garlic, and served on warm lozenges of grilled polenta.

TOMATO AND OREGANO CROSTINI

In the summer months, I like to keep things simple and tend to make my cichèti at home using only a few excellent ingredients. There is an inverse relationship between the quality of your raw materials and preparation time (when ingredients are the absolute best you can get, you need to do very little to them) so these tomato and oregano crostini are a fitting expression of the season and its bounty. They also marry perfectly with any of the bitters in any of the preceding preparations.

Bar snacks for 6–10

500g (1lb 2oz) excellent, small, ripe tomatoes
Large handful of fresh oregano leaves, stalks removed
Extra virgin olive oil
1 white baguette, sliced into approximately 20 elliptical discs, 2cm (¾in) thick
1 garlic clove, peeled
Flaky sea salt and freshly ground black pepper

Give yourself plenty of space with a large chopping board and a very sharp or serrated knife. Cut the tomatoes into pieces, about the size of small dice. Shape isn't important, but creating as much surface area as possible is key. Discard the stalky bits from the crown but keep the seeds and juice, of which there should be plenty. Transfer the chopped tomatoes into a large bowl and scatter over a generous amount of salt. Leave to stand for at least 20 minutes, preferably in sunlight.

Tear any large leaves of oregano in half and add to the tomatoes with a good glug of olive oil. Stir once or twice. Keep the small oregano leaves intact and set aside.

Grill the slices of baguette until they are lightly charred but still have a little spring when pressed with a finger. (If you have a barbecue on the go, even better. A few minutes over hot coals does wonders for the flavour.) Rub the garlic clove once only on to one side of each slice. Arrange on a large platter. Taste the tomatoes and add more salt if necessary, then spoon generously over the grilled bread. Scatter the remaining small oregano leaves evenly with a twist of black pepper and a drizzle of olive oil, then serve with a bitter aperitivo of your choice.

Rogue Fruit
by Tamar Adler

I once came across a passage in a strange, antiquarian American fruit growers' manual, a book I was reading because the names in it were so good – Green Seek-no-further, Neversink, Skinner's Superb – and it became a kind of runic mantra: 'Our garden varieties of fruits are not natural forms. They are the artificial productions of culture. Seedlings from them have always a tendency to improve, but they have also another and a stronger *tendency to return to a natural or wild state.'* What stuck with me was the idea that a fruit is always attempting to secede.

I don't know how better to describe wildness than what we haven't pinned down or reverse engineered. That description of all fruit arching towards the unpinnable is enough for me. Fruit is trying to escape.

There's another book, *The Anatomy of Dessert,* about the old English tradition of having a fruit course after the pastry or pudding. A decorous ceremony you could all do together. It's to the book's credit that it includes wine pairings. The assertion that 'the nomenclature of flavour is more scanty than even that of colour' set up my whole philosophy of fruit. To put a fine point on it, not only is fruit mounting a mutiny; it evades description.

Fruit is weird.

Here are the best and fruitiest fruits I've enjoyed recently, in the order in which they came to mind: frozen dehydrated peaches from my father-in-law's freezer; mandarins peeled and segmented in the morning, then forgotten and eaten five hours later once they'd developed a fine, brittle shell; a grapefruit I stole only a few years ago, from a large sandy orchard in Israel, mostly to shock my mother; a lot of figs about 30 minutes from rotting in a Sonoma farmers' market that thankfully had a bathroom; a deflated, misshapen apple in the back seat of a Basque farmer's car as we sped along country roads towards a restaurant where lunch was cooked on old vines and applewood. It was the best apple I've ever had.

People talk about the perfect peach. But the idea eludes my comprehension entirely. I can't imagine a perfect peach. The whole idea is stressful. But find me a fruit that's trying to rebel and I'll find a way to run into it – too many seeds, a citrus skin too thick to peel, an apple that lasts unreasonably long, its flavour concentrating. Give me an unpredictable, misshapen peach. You've got my attention.

Boozy Fruit

In *The Anatomy of Dessert*, published in 1929, pomologist and epicure Edward Bunyard offered advice on the most delightful fruit and wine pairings – 'two excellent creatures… long been regarded as suitable companions'. Here are a few of his 'experiments in match-making':

- Apples: dry port or sherry
- Apricots: sweet wine, such as Sauternes or Monbazillac
- Figs: sherry or Marsala – 'a few drops of either, inserted with an eye-dropper into the fruit before serving will win much applause'
- Gooseberries: a Moselle
- Melons: almost any wine – 'it would seem that an unsuitable wedding is hardly possible'
- Strawberries: claret or Beaujolais

In *The Book of St John*, Fergus Henderson and Trevor Gulliver suggest that strawberries would be better paired with something pink and sparkling: 'Submerge the strawberries in your bubbles of choice and refrigerate overnight. As time passes the strawberries and wine transfer their goodness to one another: a mutually beneficial arrangement.'

Diana Henry is equally enamoured of boozy fruit, preferring it above most desserts and even naming her book – *How to Eat a Peach* – after the enlightening experience of seeing white peaches dropped into glasses of cold Moscato on her maiden trip to Italy: 'I was bowled over that something this simple was considered as desirable as a slaved-over bit of patisserie.' Her recommendations include:

- Cherries soaked in Valpolicella or Pinot Noir with cardamom cream and rose pistachio shortbread
- Raspberries, blackberries and figs in late-harvest Riesling, served with a simple almond or hazelnut cake
- White nectarines and raspberries dropped into glasses of rosé

The wine must be sweetened to turn these simple pairings into refined desserts, gently simmered with sugar and then chilled, perhaps poaching the firmer fruit so it softens and yields. Elegant puddings for sultry summer evenings.

A Menu for July

by Selina Periampillai

COCONUT FISH SKEWERS WITH LIME

Grilled or barbecued fish is popular around the Indian Ocean islands; outdoor cooking of fresh fish sourced that morning is a regular sight, normally stuffed with herbs, spices and coconut. The coconut crust in this recipe adds texture to the fish and helps it to stay together. With its golden turmeric hue and mellow coconut-milk marinade, this dish is perfect for a summer's evening paired with tomato and chilli salsa.

Serves 4

4 wooden skewers, soaked in water
500g (1lb 2oz) firm white fish (cod, haddock), cut into chunks
400ml (14fl oz) coconut milk
5cm (2in) piece of fresh ginger, grated
1 tsp chilli flakes
2 garlic cloves, finely minced
Juice of 1 lime
½ tsp ground turmeric
6 tbsp desiccated coconut
Extra virgin olive oil, to drizzle
Sea salt and freshly ground black pepper
Cooked basmati rice, to serve

In a bowl, combine the fish with the coconut milk, ginger, chilli, garlic, lime juice and turmeric. Season with salt and pepper. Mix well and leave to marinate for 10 minutes.

Take the skewers out of the water and thread them through the pieces of fish – about five pieces per skewer.

Scatter the desiccated coconut on to a plate. Lift each skewer, holding it at the ends, and press it into the coconut. Make sure all sides of the fish are covered. Drizzle with olive oil and place the fish under a preheated grill, on a griddle or on the barbecue. Cook for around 3 minutes on each side, until the fish is opaque and cooked throughout. Serve immediately alongside fluffy basmati rice and Mauritian tomato and chilli salsa.

MAURITIAN TOMATO AND CHILLI SALSA

A versatile salsa that pairs perfectly with fish or chicken dishes straight off the grill or barbecue.

Serves 4

2 medium tomatoes, finely chopped
½ large mango, diced
½ small red onion, finely chopped
1 bird's eye chilli, finely chopped
A few coriander (cilantro) sprigs, roughly chopped
2 tbsp extra virgin olive oil, to drizzle
Juice of ½ lime
Sea salt and freshly ground black pepper

Toss together the tomatoes, mango, onion, chilli and coriander in a mixing bowl. Pop into the fridge and chill until serving. When ready to serve, dress with olive oil and lime juice and season to taste.

PINEAPPLE AND CHILLI SORBET

The combination of chilli and fruit is reminiscent of a popular beach-side snack in Mauritius, where pineapple is marinated with red chilli, tangy tamarind and sea salt. Transforming this into a sorbet results in a refreshing hot-cold sensory treat.

Serves 4-6

200g (7oz) caster (superfine) sugar
50ml (2fl oz) water
1 red chilli, halved, stalk removed
500g (1lb 2oz) pineapple flesh
Lime wedges and mint sprigs, to serve

Place the sugar, water and chilli in a non-stick pan over a medium heat. Simmer for 5 minutes until the sugar has dissolved and the syrup has thickened slightly. Remove from the heat and set aside to cool.

Place the pineapple in a blender with the cooled sugar syrup and whizz until a smooth purée is formed. Pour into a non-metallic container, cover and freeze for 2 hours. Remove from the freezer and use a fork to break up the crystals (this helps create a smoother result), then return to the freezer for 2–4 hours. Remove from the freezer 10 minutes before serving.

Place 1–2 scoops into a bowl or glass and decorate with a lime wedge and mint sprig.

Reading List

Jane Grigson, *Fruit Book*
At first glance, simply an alphabetical guide to fruit. On closer inspection, an imaginative compendium of recipes that weaves fragments of history and poetry into pithy prose. Essential reading, along with Grigson's *Vegetable Book*.

Mark Diacono, *Sour*
The definitive cookbook on the magical element that can transform your cooking, from kimchi to kefir, citrus to sourdough.

**Tamar Adler,
*An Everlasting Meal***
A meditation on cooking and eating, inspired by M.F.K. Fisher's *How to Cook a Wolf*, with thought-provoking ideas and practical advice that demonstrate the implicit frugality in cooking.

**Edward Bunyard,
*The Anatomy of Dessert***
A classic work, first published in 1929, and a delectable paean to fruit. Quirky and entertaining.

Russell Norman, *Venice*
An intimate glimpse into the life of the city – its history, secret places, daily life and the food that makes Venice so vibrant.

Talia Baiocchi and Leslie Pariseau, *Spritz*
The surprising history of the aperitivo and an introduction to a style of drinking that has become synonymous with the leisurely, convivial golden hour.

**Selina Periampillai,
*The Island Kitchen***
Recipes that will transport you to the warm, welcoming kitchens of the Indian Ocean islands.

August

THE COOK'S LARDER

Ingredients to look out for in August:

- Loganberries, melons, mulberries, redcurrants, whitecurrants
- Aubergine, broccoli, courgette, fennel, marsh samphire, runner beans
- Bilberries, chicken of the woods, rowan berries, summer truffles, wild angelica
- Buffalo mozzarella, burrata, Rocamadour

Summer holidays are here and there's a carefree nature
to the way people move and talk. Now is the time for
barbecues and impromptu park gatherings, or trips to the
seaside for ice cream and wind-whipped hair. Beach food
can be anything at all as long as you can eat it with your
hands, the sea air salting your food as you bite. England
excels at seaside snacks: crab sandwiches, fish and chips,
pots of cockles with a vinegar punch, candy floss on the
pier and hot sugared doughnuts burning fingers through
oil-stained paper bags.

Josceline Dimbleby suggests 'baps stuffed with grated
cheese, slivered onions and herbs, wrapped in foil and
heated in the oven... still warm and lusciously gooey',
a sensible idea when you consider the fickle nature
of British weather. Stroll to sun-faded awnings to
eat locally caught shellfish straight from the sea –
shrimps, cockles, mussels, crabs – their briny sweetness
instantly addictive.

At home, simmer shellfish in heavily salted water
(seawater, if you can get it) and, once it has cooled,
serve as simply as possible: with brown bread and butter,
lemon wedges and perhaps a homemade mayonnaise, whisked by
hand until it wobbles and shines. A platter of seafood,
or *fruits de mer* as the French romantically call it,
doesn't need to be reserved for holidays and extravagant
restaurant experiences. Rick Stein suggests it as 'a
wonderful dish for a leisurely outdoor lunch by the sea on
a hot summer's day, with plenty of chilled white wine and
nothing else to do but sit and pick and chat'. Bliss.

Samphire

A PLANT WORTH ITS SALT

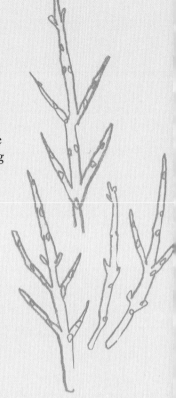

With its bright green fleshy fronds, samphire looks like a miniature succulent. It tastes of the sea – unsurprising as it thrives around tidal creeks and wetlands – and is only in season during the summer months.

Marsh samphire has become a prized ingredient in recent years, lauded by chefs and home cooks alike, but this hasn't always been the case. The Victorians considered it an inferior substitute for rock samphire, which grows high above the water and was often pickled like gherkins. Now the tide has turned, and it's marsh samphire you'll find at your local fishmonger, and even on the supermarket fish counter. It may be easy to buy, but on a sunny day by the sea it's fun to pull on your wellington boots and forage for your own. Pick with care and use scissors to cut the stems (it's illegal to uproot them).

Samphire can be eaten raw but it's better to blanch it to get rid of some of the saltiness, or fry it gently in unsalted butter. Whatever you do, make it brief so as to retain the distinctive crispness. A squeeze of lemon won't go amiss. As you'd expect, samphire pairs perfectly with fish, but it also works with lamb, in salads, tossed with spaghetti, or even as a garnish in a gin and tonic.

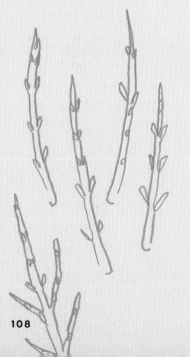

GLASS ACT

Marsh samphire is sometimes called glasswort, a name that goes back to the 16th century and is thought to refer to the use of its ashes in glass-making.

The Arrival
by Yomi Sode

Any second now, Mummy Biyi will turn up the music, leave the
garden and say *not too long my dear, until he is with us*. In
the kitchen, Uncle Peters prances up and down with his chilled
Guinness in hand. The growl in his stomach serving as a soundtrack
to his militant walk. The aunties cut their eye and sing as I
unfurl layers of cling film off each plastic bowl containing Fish
and Beef. Mummy Biyi's kitchen soon becomes a place of worship
and nostalgia.

As children, when we wished for summer to never end and the sun,
a talking drum of heat beating our Black backs — Biyi and I
swapped whimsical fire hydrants for sprinklers in Aunty's garden.
Running into the cool until it became unbearable, then running out
until the heat became too much to handle. No middle ground for our
bodies to find peace. *Not too long my dear, until he is with us*.

I watch mum spread chicken pieces on a chopping board. They look
like a row of cards, seasoned with Maggi, curry powder, onions and
peppers. She rubs seasoning into each piece with her bare hands.
This must be where healing takes place in the absence of chivalry
and separately, as if by clockwork — a crescendo of clanking pans
and sizzle happen. A firework of oils pop in the air. Mummy Biyi
ferociously spins a tea towel underneath the fire alarm like a
propeller while Uncle Peters follows the scent into the kitchen
and the untimely presence of a flustered wife, who vows to strike
and starve the men at the next gathering!

Every year, I look forward to Biyi arriving home, amid the chaos
and love. That's the point I know the rest will soon join after.
Aunty Biyi cooked her trinity of Jollof, Fried and Plain rice
as standard servings, a selection of swallow food (*iyan*, *eba*,
amala). And lastly, stews (*egusi*, *efo riro* and *omi obe*) for the
more traditional eaters. Food, to my family, is like book spines
to readers. Mummy Biyi begins to pray, she welcomes the family for
another year as we wait for them to arrive. I mouth amen while my
mind wonders. This is the last summer I'll be with them, waiting.

Next year, they will be waiting for me to arrive. *Amin, ni oruko jesu!* And just like that, the front door opens. We peer through the passage at two suitcases stacked on top of each other. At Biyi, looking tired but grateful. Aunty soon turns to me, *my boy is home*.

DAWADAWA SEARED SCALLOPS
by Zoe Adjonyoh

Dawadawa is fermented locust bean, also known as *iru*, a traditional condiment in Nigeria that comes in a paste or as a ground powder. The heady smell is off-putting to some but its deep umami taste is a winner every time. It's an amazing ingredient for recipes where fish or seafood is a component and it adds a nuanced flavour of fish to vegetarian or vegan dishes.

This recipe makes a great canapé or starter to wow dinner party guests: it sings of West African flavour loud and proud. While there are a few steps to follow, it's not at all complicated and as a bonus you get to make your main dish – *efo riro* – at the same time. Choose your side: fried plantain, pounded yam or plain boiled rice.

Serves 4-6

For the spice mix:
1 tsp ground smoked crayfish
½ tsp ground dawadawa
½ tbsp ground ginger
1 tsp garlic powder
1 tsp dried red chilli flakes
½ tsp dried thyme
¼ tsp ground cinnamon
½ tsp ground nutmeg
1 tsp ground coriander
1 tbsp freshly chopped flat-leaf parsley (optional)

450–550g (1lb 4oz) scallops (approximately 12–16)
2 tsp unsalted butter
2 tsp olive oil
Microgreens, to garnish

Blend together the spice mix ingredients in a spice grinder or pestle and mortar.

Remove any side muscle from the scallops, rinse with cold water and pat dry. Coat the scallops in the spice mix, cover and refrigerate for 25 minutes. Remove from the fridge 5 minutes before cooking to let the scallops return to room temperature.

Heat the butter and oil in a sauté pan on a medium-high heat. Season the scallops before searing them for 1–2 minutes on each side. You should see a lovely golden crust start to form while the centre of the scallop remains translucent.

Garnish with microgreens, such as red-veined sorrel and serve immediately.

You can stop right there and you've got yourself a banging dish. But to make it extra special, serve your scallops atop a gorgeous pile of efo riro and you'll have West African surf and turf at its finest.

EFO RIRO

```
For the spice paste:
4 red (bell) peppers, roughly chopped
1 medium onion, roughly chopped
2 Scotch bonnet or 3 habanero chillies

450-750g (1-1⅔lb) chopped fresh spinach
235ml (8fl oz) palm oil
450g (1lb) goat meat or braising steak, diced
1 medium onion, finely diced
2 tbsp ground smoked crayfish
100-120g (3½oz) red prawns, cleaned and heads removed
450g (1lb) washed and deboned shredded smoked fish
(catfish or mackerel)
1 tbsp ground dawadawa
```

For the spice paste, blend the red peppers, onion and chillies until smooth, then pass the mixture through a muslin cloth to remove excess liquid.

Place the spinach in a bowl and add 1 teaspoon of salt. Allow to rest for 20 minutes. Rinse the spinach and squeeze out the excess water.

Place a large heavy-based pot over a medium-low heat and add the palm oil. When the oil starts to have a smokey aroma, add the diced goat or beef and seal it on all sides. Remove from the pan, drain any excess oil and set aside.

In the same pan, sauté the diced onion until lightly browned and add the spice paste. Gently stir before adding the remaining ingredients, including the goat or beef, but not the spinach. Cover and leave to simmer for 90 minutes or until the palm oil rises to the top of the sauce.

Add the rinsed spinach. Stir, taste and adjust for seasoning, then leave to simmer for another 5 minutes, until the spinach has wilted.

The End of the Pier

by Jessica Andrews

I was sealed shut for a long time. I was tucked tightly inside of myself, afraid of letting anyone get close. That summer the lid came off and the sky fell in. Sometimes I had to stop in the middle of the street to catch my breath.

'Let's get out of the city,' you said, so we did. We took a train to the nearest beach, then threw down our dirty tote bags and ran across the sand, gulping emerald and brine. We followed the edge of the water, picking up pink shells and frosted chunks of sea glass. The wind pulled the hair away from my face. I closed my eyes and let it rush through me.

At the end of the pier there was a small white cabin, sun-bleached and rusted by sea spray. Rows of cockles glistered in the pale light.

'Do you like crab?' you asked with your eyes on my lips. I liked the word 'crab' in your mouth with its hard, scuttling consonants, but I hadn't eaten it since I was a child; a flower of claws on a paper plate, arranged by an auntie at a party. You were the first person who taught me to see an appetite as a cause for celebration instead of something shameful. I wanted to impress you with my hunger, my capacity for pleasure.

'I can't remember,' I said, truthfully.

'Really?' Your eyes were bright as you moved towards the counter. 'Can we have a crab?' A woman in white latex gloves and coral-coloured lipstick nodded. You

pulled me towards you. 'Let's watch her dress it.'

I watched the woman's gloved hands remove the legs with a twist and a soft snap. She pushed out the crab's stomach and I felt aware of the hot weight of my heart in my chest. She pressed her knuckles into its strange body.

'She's looking for the witch's fingers,' you whispered, your hand on the back of my neck.

'The what?'

'The bad parts. The bits you can't eat.' I swallowed as the woman scraped the meat from its shell and you pinched the small of my back. She rubbed salt between her finger and thumb, sprinkled parsley, squeezed lemon.

'Mayo?' She glanced up. You waited for me to answer.

'Yes, please.'

We sat with our legs dangling over the water. The sun was ripe on my bare shoulders. I scooped the meat with a wooden fork and it fell apart on my tongue. It was silt and cream and softness. It tasted of velvet and the bottom of the sea. It was the worry beneath my bones and the salt in your skin, so delicate that it scared me.

'Well?' You looked at me.

'Yeah. Delicious.' I cast the empty shell into the waves and watched it disappear.

A Menu for August

by Alex Jackson

SOCCA AND CRAB

This is a good thing to eat on a warm summer's day with a cold drink in hand. Socca is the Niçoise version of Liguria's favourite *farinata*: a chickpea flour crêpe traditionally baked in a wood oven. Unfortunately, I don't have a wood oven, so I tend to think of socca less as a pancake and more as a fritter. The ideal socca should be hot, thin and crisp on both sides, yet pleasingly soft within. It's traditionally served unadorned, sprinkled with nothing but flaky salt and ground black pepper. That is fine, of course, but here there is a harmonious contrast: a hot, plain chickpea fritter topped with rich, cool crab.

For the socca:
200g (7oz) chickpea flour
360ml (12fl oz) water
1 tbsp olive oil, plus extra for frying
1 small rosemary sprig
Flaky sea salt

For the crab:
50g (1¾oz) picked white crab meat
1 tbsp olive oil
2 tsp finely chopped parsley
2 tsp crème fraîche
Lemon juice, to taste
Sea salt and freshly ground black pepper

Sift the chickpea flour into a bowl and slowly whisk in the water. Be careful to beat out any lumps. Whisk in the olive oil. The batter should be the thickness of single cream. Leave to stand, covered, in the fridge for at least a few hours or, better, overnight.

Preheat the grill.

In a bowl, mix all the ingredients for the crab together. Season to taste with lemon juice, salt and pepper. Keep chilled in the fridge.

Heat a non-stick pan over a high heat until very hot. Add sufficient olive oil to

cover the whole pan. As the oil begins to smoke, slowly pour in your chickpea batter. The batter should be no more than about 2mm deep, like a thick crêpe. The oil will fizz up and the batter will start to bubble around the edges. Pick the leaves off the rosemary sprig and scatter some on to the batter. Cook for a minute on a medium heat to crisp up the bottom.

Place the socca in the pan under the hot grill until golden brown and crispy, but still a little soft inside. It may catch slightly in places, but this is to be encouraged.

Cut the socca into quarters or sixths. Sprinkle with flaky sea salt, top with as much of the seasoned crab as you think your slice can carry, and eat hot. Repeat until you have eaten your fill or until all the batter is used up.

ROAST HAKE, SAMPHIRE AND TOMATO SALAD

Samphire and tomatoes are where British food meets its Mediterranean counterpart. The two ingredients go together very well, especially when dressed with plenty of herbs, lemon juice and olive oil. Both have a pleasing juicy succulence going on. Samphire and tomatoes pair well with any fish. Grilled oily sardines or mackerel would be great, but here I've chosen a piece of firm hake, which flakes nicely into the salad. The fish is roasted on the bone over a bed of herbs with a little wine. Cooking it this way ensures the moist flesh can be eased off the bone. This is especially delicious served with a generous blob of mayonnaise or aioli.

Serves 4

A fat piece of hake or any other flaky white fish, on the bone, weighing approximately 1kg (2lb 4oz)
2 tbsp olive oil, plus extra for dressing
Sprigs of rosemary, thyme, bay and tarragon, for a bed of herbs
1 unwaxed lemon, ½ sliced into rounds, ½ for juicing
200ml (7fl oz) dry white wine
1 tbsp butter
4 large, juicy tomatoes
100g (3½oz) samphire, washed
1 tbsp each parsley and tarragon leaves, roughly chopped
Sea salt and freshly ground black pepper

Preheat the oven to 200°C/400°F/gas mark 6.

Select an appropriately sized roasting dish for the fish: it needs to be a snug fit. Drizzle the dish with olive oil and build a bed of herbs. Season the hake with salt and pepper both inside and out. Nestle the fish in the herbs, slide a few slices of lemon inside the fish with some tarragon stalks too. Pour over the wine, drizzle liberally with olive oil, then dot the fish with butter.

Roast for 20 minutes, or until the flesh offers very little resistance when pierced to the bone with a skewer. It's best to remove the fish from the oven when it is almost cooked as it will continue to steam and cook on the bone while you assemble the rest of the dish. If the wine threatens to boil away during cooking, add a splash of water. Ideally there will be some buttery, winey juices left in the bottom of the dish.

To bring it all together, cut the tomatoes into fat chunks, then season with salt and pepper. Fill a large pan with water and bring to the boil. Cook the samphire in the boiling water for only a minute or two, or until soft and succulent. (Do not add salt.) Drain and set aside. Combine the tomatoes with the samphire, while it's still warm, and dress with olive oil, the lemon juice and chopped herbs.

Arrange the still-warm tomato and samphire salad on a serving platter. Flake the hake flesh off the bone in big pieces and lay them just to the side of the salad. Drizzle any buttery, winey juices from the roasting dish over the fish.

A crusty baguette would do a first-class job of mopping up the juices here, making an impromptu open sandwich of warm, buttery fish and juicy tomatoes.

PANNA COTTA AND CHERRIES POACHED IN PASTIS

Poaching cherries in pastis results in a deep, dark crimson liquid. Sweet, sour and with a heady aniseed hit, it's something syrupy, exotic and vivid to pour around your white vanilla-speckled set cream. Any leftover cherry liquor is a treat when mixed with some Crémant (or Champagne, darling) for a sort of southern Kir Royale.

Makes 4 (generous) portions

For the panna cotta:
600ml (1 pint) double (heavy) cream
1 vanilla pod or 1 tsp vanilla extract, preferably one with little black seeds in it
Rind of ½ unwaxed lemon, peeled with a vegetable peeler
1½ leaves of gelatine
75ml (2½fl oz) full-fat milk
75g (2½oz) icing (confectioners') sugar

For the poached cherries:
100ml (3½fl oz) pastis
100ml (3½fl oz) water
50g (1¾oz) caster (superfine) sugar
1 thyme sprig
400g (14oz) finest dark red cherries, stalks removed and pitted

Pour 450ml (16fl oz) of the cream into a pan over a medium heat. Add the vanilla and lemon rind, then bring to the boil. Turn the heat down and simmer slowly for a few minutes. Remove the lemon rind. If using real vanilla, remove the vanilla pod, split it lengthways and scrape the seeds back into the cream.

Soak the gelatine in the cold milk for about 15 minutes or until soft. Remove the gelatine, bring the milk to a boil, then return the gelatine to the milk and stir until dissolved. Pour the milk and gelatine mixture through a sieve into the hot cream, stir, then allow to cool. Lightly whip the remaining cream with the icing sugar and fold into the cooled cooked cream.

Pour the panna cotta mixture into your preferred moulds. I like to use individual dariole moulds that are wider than they are tall, as it makes for a prettier plate when turned out, but you can use anything you have to hand. They should be approximately 150ml (5fl oz) capacity, but make do with what you have. Leave the panna cotta in the refrigerator to set for at least 2 hours.

To poach the cherries, bring the pastis, water and sugar to the boil with the thyme sprig. Add the cherries. Cook at a low simmer for about 10–15 minutes, until the cherries have softened slightly and the poaching liquor has turned a deep red. Remove from the heat and allow the cherries to cool in the liquid. Refrigerate until cool.

To turn out the panna cotta, dip the moulds into a pot of boiling water for just a second or two. This will melt the very outside of the panna cotta and allow it to slip easily from the mould. Turn out each panna cotta into a shallow bowl, then spoon over the cherries and some of the crimson liquor.

Reading List

John Wright,
Edible Seashore
The seashore offers surprising culinary potential. A River Cottage handbook with practical advice on harvesting, cooking and conservation.

Rick Stein,
English Seafood Cookery
A classic cookbook with all the seafood recipes and advice you could want, plus tips for foraging for coastal wild foods.

Yemisi Aribisala,
Longthroat Memoirs
Essays examining the complexities, peculiarities, meticulousness and tactility of Nigerian food.

Zoe Adjonyoh,
Zoe's Ghana Kitchen
Recipes and stories that celebrate the flavours and ingredients of West Africa. Try the beef suya kebab grilled on the barbecue.

Jessica Andrews, *Saltwater*
A lyrical and boundary-breaking debut novel exploring familial bonds, class identity and the way we connect with the landscape around us.

Cynthia Nims, *Crab*
A cookbook for fans of the clawed crustacean with recipes and tips for perfectly prepared crab cakes, steamed Dungeness straight from the shell, soufflés, sandwiches, noodles and wontons.

Alex Jackson, *Sardine*
A joyous collection of recipes capturing the beauty and simplicity of Provençal cooking, with 'Grande Bouffe' menus for celebratory feasts.

September

THE COOK'S LARDER

Ingredients to look out for in September:

- Blackberries, damsons, figs, greengages, raspberries
- Chanterelles, chard, chilli, marrows, peppers, sweetcorn, tomatillos, tomatoes
- Bullace, cobnuts, crab apples, elderberries, hazelnuts, lingonberries, rosehips, sea buckthorn
- Goose
- Abondance, Fontina, Gorgonzola Dolce

The memory of summer lingers throughout September, the days balmy and clear before the soft slip into autumn. After the languor of summer holidays, this is the month for a fresh start — a renewed vigour before the merry distraction of festivities at the end of the year.

After bathing in the sun for a few glorious months, summer vegetables are at their peak. For the cook, there's a flurry of kitchen activity to capture the essence of high harvest, bottling the summer bounty for less plentiful times of year. Tomatoes have ripened to a gaudy ruby-red and need only a drizzle of olive oil to make a fine salad. 'In all of vegetabledom there is nothing to equal the tomato,' declared the American food writer Craig Claiborne, and it's tempting to eat them with every meal while they're so deliciously sweet-sharp. Look for tomatoes with character — bulbous and misshapen with folds and furrows — rather than dull uniformity. A late summer luxury.

Nothing captures the flavour of the changing season quite as much as plums. Fill your fruit bowl with dusty shades of purple, yellow and green. Poach halved and stoned plums in a little sugar and watch them collapse gracefully into soft and yielding fruit, then serve hot with a jug of cream. Prunes have a bad reputation — 'the true spirit of gastronomic joylessness' according to E.M. Forster — but plump Agen prunes are a treat, served with roast pork or goose, baked into cakes and tarts, or soaked in something deliciously boozy.

Dark berries usher in the autumnal foraging season — look for crab apples, cobnuts and rosehips, too — and late-variety raspberries join the fray. Eat them straight from the punnet while sitting outside, accompanied, perhaps, by a glass of muscat or late-harvest Riesling, and enjoy the last wisps of summer.

Corn

THE GRAIN THAT CHANGED THE WORLD

When Columbus sailed the *Santa María* to the edge of the world in 1492, it was not the gold, silver and pearls the explorers plundered that would change the course of history, but the foods they brought back across the Atlantic: potatoes, tomatoes, cocoa, chillies and corn.

Corn travelled quickly around the world, growing easily in different soils and climates. What began as a garden curiosity was soon a valuable source of food throughout southern Europe, north Africa, China and the Philippines. First cultivated around 9,000 years ago in Mexico, corn was domesticated from an ancient grass called *teosinte*. Tortillas, tamales and gruels like hominy grits are the closest surviving links to the prehistoric foods people ate in the Americas, and early preparations are still eaten all over the world, from Italian polenta to Brazilian angu, Romanian mamaliga to South African mealie.

Fresh sweetcorn came relatively late to the table. The American geneticist John Laughnan developed a 'supersweet' variety in the 1950s, which was picked fresh and eaten as a vegetable. The special elongated serving dishes, small-pronged handles and corn paraphernalia manufactured around this time show there was great enthusiasm for it.

A good corn-on-the-cob, boiled and buttered, is the definition of a simple pleasure. 'Butter it must have, plenty of it,' declared Jane Grigson, 'to bathe the yellow grains and dribble down one's chin.' Freshness matters – once picked, the sugars soon turn to starch – and choose cobs with the husk intact: they start to dry out as soon as they are disrobed. Chiselled off the cob, sweetcorn kernels bring texture and sweetness to chowders, fritters, salsas and salads; alternatively, purée them and serve with grilled fish, scallops, chicken or steak.

And let's not forget the joy of popcorn. Betty Fussell dedicates a whole chapter to it in her exhaustive study, *The Story of Corn*, revealing that our favourite cinema snack has been eaten for thousands of years: popcorn poppers dating back to the 1st century have been discovered in Peru. Who knew so much history could be contained in a kernel of corn.

Walk on the Wild Side

AUTUMN FORAGING

SEA BUCKTHORN

Look for narrow, silvery leaves and bright orange berries along the coast. Pick with care – the berries burst easily – then cook gently to release the juice. Tart with a sherbet tang, it makes a good dressing, or a daily tonic.

ROSEHIPS

Pick when the hips turn a bright red and make a syrup to pour over pancakes, panna cotta or ice cream. They're particularly good in cocktails – swap with tomato juice to make a Bloody Rosie – or infused in vodka with a little sugar.

HAZELNUTS

Woodland edges and farm hedges are the best places to find ripe nuts. When fresh, they are crisp with a hint of sweetness, but they're more versatile when dried – add to salads, stuffings, cakes and biscuits.

ELDERBERRIES

The purple-black berries that form once the white sprays of elderflowers have faded are an overlooked ingredient. Pickle them, turn into cordial or wine, add to fruit crumbles and pies, or use to make a type of Worcestershire sauce called pontac.

BULLACE

Wild plums need a little more sugar than their cultivated cousins but can be used in the same way. Cobblers and crumbles are a good place to start but, for something longer-lasting, make a fruit paste akin to membrillo to serve with cheese.

Crab Apples
by Raymond Blanc

Wrapped around the archways that frame the pathways through my orchard, our crab apple trees create their own spectacle. First, it is their blossom that captivates me. From gentle pinks to vibrant reds they are a celebration of spring. And the apples that follow are just as eye-catching in their shades of yellow, gold, orange, crimson and almost purple. I have even created a new garden for them, interplanted with large purple clematis, across from the wildflower garden, where the abundance of their foliage creates a privacy reminiscent of the romantic, secluded orchards of Shakespeare's day. Their blossom offers the bees a rich source of pollen, and this happy chef has a wonderful source of fruit for crab apple petits fours.

At Le Manoir aux Quat'Saisons we have planted five very different but beautiful varieties of crab apple: Golden Hornet, Robusta, Red Sentinel, Gorgeous and John Downie.

These wonderful, tiny, tangy ancient fruits are so much a part of our orchard heritage, woven into ancient folklore, magic and myth. It was said that if you threw the pips of a crab apple into the fire while saying the name of your love and the pips exploded, then your love would be true.

Medieval orchards consisted mainly of crab apples, along with some cultivated apples, and wild and cultivated pears. Grown from pips or cuttings, they were good pollinators and produced hardy apples for cider or for fermenting to make verjuice, which was taken as a tonic, or used as a souring agent in cooking. They were most popular roasted and served in bowls of hot ale, sugar and spice at Christmastime, or for the Wassail Bowl, which would be passed around as part of the ancient tradition of blessing apple trees on Twelfth Night, a ceremony to ensure a successful year.

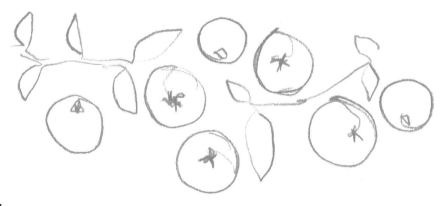

BAKED CARAMELISED CRAB APPLES

I have created these beautiful autumnal petits fours as a celebration of the season. The apples are simply baked, then coated in caramel infused with a little ginger and lime, and encrusted in nuts. Chilled first to set the caramel, then served at room temperature, they are delightful little treats to serve to your friends at the end of dinner.

Makes 12 petits fours

12 small crab apples
50g (1¾oz) caster (superfine) sugar
25g (1oz) unsalted butter, cubed
25ml (1fl oz) lime juice
Pinch of salt
½ tsp finely grated fresh ginger
1 tsp pistachio nuts, roughly chopped
1 tsp nibbed almonds

Preheat the oven to 180°C/350°F/gas mark 4.

Arrange the crab apples upright in a heavy-based oven tray. Bake for 25 minutes until the apples are cooked through and soft, but still hold their shape.

In a medium saucepan on a medium heat, bring the caster sugar to a blond caramel. Remove from the heat, carefully add the butter and move the pan to allow the liquid to swirl around and cool down, to prevent it from caramelising further.

Add the lime juice, salt and ginger, return the pan to the heat and simmer until you have a thick caramel that will coat the back of a spoon. Take off the heat and allow to cool slightly.

Line a clean tray with baking paper. Holding each of the crab apples by its stalk, dip into the caramel sauce, and place on the lined tray. Sprinkle with the chopped pistachios and nibbed almonds and put in the fridge for 30 minutes.

Remove from the fridge and allow the apples to return to room temperature before serving.

The Best Figs I Ever Had

by Itamar Srulovich

When Adam Kindred, the protagonist in William Boyd's novel *Ordinary Thunderstorms*, suddenly finds himself down and out and hustling to survive among London's dispossessed, he seeks shelter in an overgrown patch of land on Chelsea Embankment. I recognised the place immediately as I rode on the 452 bus from my home in Battersea to Notting Hill, where I worked as a chef at the time. I noticed that scrappy patch of land because of a large fig tree that grew there. I always notice fig trees: they signal good luck for me.

I was so happy to see that tree, with its gnarled branches and broad leaves shaping a generous canopy. It was like seeing a familiar face, a friend from home. Like me, it came from warmer climes, and it gave me hope to see it thriving on the bank of the Thames. I could see why this would be the place to seek safety if everything suddenly went wrong, as it does for Adam in Boyd's novel.

There was a fig tree in the garden of the house in which I grew up in Jerusalem, and two massive trees in the schoolyard, which were in full fruit in September when the school year started. Their fruit sweetened the bitterness we felt at the end of the summer holidays. As we got older this was where we came to hang out, smoke, make out, get high. All of our teen dramas were played out under that wide canopy, with that particular smell emanating from the leaves – like resin, or petrol, a little bit like coconut – enveloping all of our youthful misadventures.

When my wife, Sarit, and I first moved into a rental together in Tel Aviv we got a little fig tree in a small oval pot, and when we moved to London two years later we gave that tree to her parents. They planted it in their garden and we love to see it every time we return. It is taller than me now, and growing strong.

In London, when looking for a place to live, after seeing dozens of flats, we met an estate agent at the entrance to a building in Stockwell. He was waiting under a fig tree – and we knew we'd arrived home. The tree officially belongs to our neighbours but they don't mind when we pick some leaves to roast a chicken in or to flavour custard for ice cream.

When we opened our deli Honey & Spice a few years ago, we had room for a planter by the entrance. It faced south and we thought it would be a good spot for a little fig tree of our own. It has done well under the care of our dear friend Bridget, the manager of the deli, and last August it produced some fruit – just three or four figs, but we were happy to see them and followed their progress through a hot September, when suddenly they changed colour and gained a purple blush.

The heat continued through the month and as the days went by there was no denying: we had ripe figs growing on Warren Street. We picked them at the end of the month, on my birthday, straight from the tree, and ate them at the tables outside with the afternoon sun in our eyes. They had that resin/petrol/little-bit-like-coconut taste. They were juicy but not the juiciest, sweet but not the sweetest, and they were the best figs I ever had.

Pimentón

THE SPICE OF SPAIN

Little smokehouses punctuate the landscape of La Vera in western Spain. In autumn, strings of red peppers picked from the surrounding fields are hung up in the rafters and smoked over smouldering holm oak fires. The peppers take on a mellow smokiness as they dry, a characteristic unique to pimentón de la Vera, and are then ground to a soft powder and packaged in pretty tins.

There are several types of pimentón, or Spanish paprika, made throughout Spain: *dulce* (sweet and mild), *agridulce* (bittersweet) and *picante* (hot). According to the chef José Pizarro, the hot version tends to be used in hearty soups and spicy chorizo. The sweet version, he says, 'has an extraordinary affinity with potatoes and firm-fleshed white meat such as octopus, rabbit and chicken', while the bittersweet pimentón accentuates game and bean stews.

A Menu for September
by José Pizarro

ANCHOVY, PIQUILLO PEPPER AND WALNUT SALAD

There's a roadside café on the main road from Madrid to Portugal – at junction 46, if you ever go that way. The place is littered with discarded paper napkins, cigarette butts and broken toothpicks. It feels like a railway station it's so busy, and you have to give the bar staff a determined stare if they're ever going to notice you. But keep trying, and make sure you ask for the *boquerones en vinagre*. They arrive (eventually), with a huge chunk of bread and no knife or fork. Don't worry, just use a toothpick and tuck into the best marinated anchovies ever: plump, covered in juicy chunks of garlic and golden olive oil. The governor of Extremadura always stops here, which tells you how good they are. These days the deli counters at better supermarkets have very acceptable anchovies, which are fine in this salad. If you can't find jars or tins of piquillo peppers, use jarred roasted red peppers instead.

Serves 4

100g (3½oz) red piquillo peppers
16 marinated anchovies
1 small red onion, finely sliced
Handful of fresh herbs, such as mint, chervil and flat-leaf parsley

For the dressing:
4 tbsp extra virgin olive oil
2 tbsp Cabernet Sauvignon red wine vinegar
40g (1½oz) toasted walnuts, broken into rough pieces
Freshly ground black pepper

First make the dressing: mix the oil, vinegar and walnuts together, and season with a couple of twists of freshly ground black pepper.

Cut the piquillo peppers into 1cm (½in) slices, then combine in a bowl with the anchovies, sliced onion and herbs. Pour over the dressing, toss and serve.

PAN-FRIED PIMENTÓN CHICKEN WITH MASHED POTATO

I prefer to use pimentón de la Vera picante for this dish, but please use it with caution! Mashed potato made with olive oil is just gorgeous with this.

Serves 4

For the chicken:
3 tbsp extra virgin olive oil
4 garlic cloves, peeled
1 bay leaf
8 boneless, skinless chicken thighs, cut in half
1 tsp pimentón de la Vera picante (hot smoked paprika)
6 tbsp Fino sherry
Sea salt and freshly ground black pepper

For the mash:
4 large red potatoes
4 garlic cloves
1 bay leaf
6 tbsp extra virgin olive oil

First, you want to infuse the oil that the chicken is going to be cooked in with the flavours of the garlic and bay leaf. So, warm the oil in a pan over a very gentle heat and add the garlic cloves and the bay leaf. It should take about 20 minutes to colour the garlic, very slightly. Once cooked, remove the garlic and bay leaf. Set the garlic aside (you'll need it later).

Turn the heat up to high. Season the chicken, add it to the pan and fry for 4 minutes before turning the pieces over – you want them to be nicely crispy and golden. Cook for another 4 minutes. Add the pimentón and the sherry; give everything a good stir and leave to bubble gently for 5 minutes.

Meanwhile, for the mash, peel the potatoes and cut them into large chunks. Boil with the garlic cloves, bay leaf, 2 tablespoons of the olive oil and a pinch of salt. Once cooked, skim off the olive oil and reserve. Drain the potatoes and remove the garlic and bay leaf. Mash the potatoes with all the olive oil (both the reserved and the remaining olive oil), and keep going until you have made a smooth purée. Season to taste.

Spoon the mashed potatoes into the middle of a platter, place the chicken on top, and pour over the juices. Serve with the fried garlic cloves.

CHOCOLATE CAKES WITH CHOCOLATE PIMENTÓN SAUCE

The smokiness of pimentón works a treat with chocolate – but you cannot cook the two together as the paprika will turn bitter, so make a sauce and stir in the spice at the last minute.

```
Serves 6

200g (7oz) plain chocolate (70% cocoa solids), chopped
120g (4¼oz) salted butter, cut into 1cm (½in) cubes
6 large egg yolks
120g (4¼oz) caster (superfine) sugar
2 large egg whites

For the chocolate pimentón sauce:
100g (3½oz) chocolate (70% cocoa solids)
3 tbsp extra virgin olive oil
⅓ tsp pimentón de la Vera dulce (mild smoked paprika)

Handful of cherries, to serve
```

Preheat the oven to 200°C/400°F/gas mark 6. Butter six 200ml (7fl oz) muffin tins or ramekins and arrange on a baking tray.

Put the chocolate and butter into a heavy saucepan and stir over a low heat until smooth. Don't let it boil. Remove from the heat and leave to cool until lukewarm, stirring occasionally.

Meanwhile, use an electric whisk to beat the egg yolks and all but 1 tablespoon of the sugar in a large bowl for about 5 minutes, until the mixture is thick and pale. Fold a tablespoon of the egg mixture into the melted chocolate, then fold this back into the remaining egg mixture in the bowl.

In another bowl, beat the egg whites until soft peaks form. Add the remaining tablespoon of sugar and continue to beat the whites until you have created firm peaks. Using a metal spoon, fold the egg whites into the chocolate mixture, then divide this equally between the muffin tins or ramekins. Bake for about 12 minutes, until the edges are set but the centres still soft. Cook for a couple of minutes longer if you want a firm middle. Remove the tins from the baking tray and cool for a couple of minutes.

For the sauce, melt the chocolate with the olive oil in a small pan over a low heat, stirring regularly. Keep warm and, just before serving, stir in the pimentón. To serve, use a knife to go round the sides of the tins to loosen the cakes, if necessary. Slip the cakes out of the tins and arrange on plates. Drizzle a little sauce over each. Serve with cherries. Eat while still warm.

Reading List

Betty Fussell,
The Story of Corn
A mesmerising account of the extraordinary grain that built the New World, blending personal narrative, social history, art, science and anthropology.

Kylee Newton,
The Modern Preserver
Recipes to preserve the summer glut, from chutney to kimchi, jam to gin. Try the pickled jalapeños recipe.

Jane Hirshfield, *After*
A poetry collection featuring 'The Heat of Autumn', a poem that captures the way summer slips into autumn.

Raymond Blanc,
The Lost Orchard
A love letter to the ancient and forgotten varieties of British apples and pears, with practical information, anecdotes from the orchards and recipes from the kitchen of the French chef's Oxfordshire restaurant.

Itamar Srulovich and Sarit Packer, *Honey & Co At Home*
Simple and delicious Middle Eastern dishes to cook at home, imbued with the warmth and sophistication of the couple's London restaurants.

José Pizarro,
Seasonal Spanish Food
Seasonal recipes, notes on ingredients and childhood stories from the Spanish chef, who grew up on a farm in Extremadura. All told with infectious enthusiasm.

October

THE COOK'S LARDER

Ingredients to look out for in October:

- Apples, grapes, pears, quince
- Borlotti beans, celeriac, pumpkin, romanesco, squash, white truffles
- Juniper, sweet chestnuts, walnuts, wild mushrooms
- Grouse
- Berkswell, Rogue River Blue, Saint-Nectaire

In October autumn truly arrives. A chill pricks the evening air and the trees silently turn to vivid shades of saffron and scarlet, their last days full of colour. On the best days there is a mellow brightness that calls you outside into the clear, crisp air to rustle through the fallen leaves. Yet as the writer P.D. James reminds us, these perfect autumnal days 'occur more frequently in memory than in life', and more often than not the creeping cold draws us inside, and into the kitchen.

A sudden drop in temperature stirs the appetite. Thick jumpers come out of the closet and hearty soups simmer on the stove. Portions must be generous: piles of hot buttered toast, deep bowls of pasta and spicy noodle soups, potatoes baked long and slow until the soft interior is encased in a perfect shell. Carbs are necessary at this time of year.

Tree fruits come into their own now, despite being on offer for most of the year. Venture out to a local farmers' market to discover apple varieties never to be seen on supermarket shelves: Blenheim Orange, Roxbury Russet, Worcester Pearmain, Ashmead's Kernel with its elusive flavour reminiscent of pear drops, and Bramleys, of course, which add a pleasing tang to pies, crumbles and cobblers. Forage for juniper berries and quinces, sweet chestnuts and cobnuts gathered from the ground and 'wet' walnuts eaten fresh from the tree.

Halloween provides a sweet end to the month, an excuse for garish excess and fanciful feasts. The origins of All Hallows' Eve are unknown to most, but its traditions hark back to ancient Celtic harvest festivals. And so, as well as the thrill of guises and ghouls, it's an excuse for gathering together and revelling in the abundant riches of autumn.

Quince

A MUCH MISTAKEN FRUIT

Quinces have a seductive history. Some suggest the serpent tempted Eve with a quince rather than an apple, and the ancient Greeks believed that quince trees sprung up wherever Aphrodite stepped when she was born from the foaming sea, forever linking the fruit with love and fertility.

We can blame the Greeks for this fruit's muddled history. They used the term 'melon' to refer to both apples and quinces, obscuring its true importance in classical literature. Yet since it was first discovered in the foothills of the Caucasus mountains, this knobbly, yellow-skinned fruit has enchanted merchants, travelling along the ancient trade routes to the Middle East, the Mediterranean and Central Asia.

Quince trees were first recorded in Britain in 1275, when King Edward I planted four of them at the Tower of London. Early recipes include tarts filled with whole quinces sprinkled with sugar and cinnamon, and liqueurs called 'ratafias'. Quinces became a common ingredient in jams, jellies, crumbles and pies, and were often served alongside rich cuts of meat.

To our modern palates, raw quince is unpleasantly hard and astringent, yet before sugar became ubiquitous and tastes changed, the fruit was eaten straight from the tree. Cooking softens and sweetens the flesh, while turning it a rather fetching golden pink or deep, dusky red.

WHAT'S IN A NAME

Most people think of quince as a paste, or *membrillo*, to be eaten with cheese. In fact, until the 18th century, the word 'marmalade' properly belonged to the quince rather than the orange (from the Portuguese word *marmelo*).

What To Do with Quince

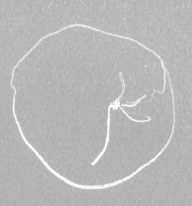

FORAGE

Look out for quinces in other people's
gardens; they may not appreciate them,
or they may be willing to share.

SCENT

A bowl of quinces will fragrance the
whole house with their heady perfume.

BAKE

Add half a quince to an apple pie to lift
the flavour, and use the purée in tarts
where you might usually use jam.

POACH

Slowly poach or stew the fruit in wine
or syrup and serve it warm with vanilla
ice cream and chopped walnuts for a
simple dessert.

PRESERVE

Pickled quince is perfect with cold
meats, pâtés, terrines and cheeses.

Soup

BOLSTERING BROTHS

Soup is cuisine's kindest course. It breathes reassurance; it steams consolation; after a weary day it promotes sociability, as the five o'clock cup of tea or the cocktail hour.
Louis P. De Gouy

Soup is a primitive dish. Since humans discovered fire and made rudimentary pots, there have been simple soups and broths to nourish and comfort. The simplest recipes are still some of the best – mulligatawny, chowder, borscht, rasam, oxtail or mutton broth, Welsh cawl – but soups don't need a recipe at all. After all, soups are the kings of leftovers.

We turn to soup for comfort and to clear our heads. Childhood favourites come to the fore – a can of Heinz Cream of Tomato should always nestle at the back of the cupboard for emergencies, ready for bread rolls to be generously buttered and eagerly dunked. Laurie Colwin, novelist and author of *Home Cooking*, one of the very best food books, wrote that 'to feel safe and warm on a cold wet night, all you really need is soup'. This is true, at least in the moment. The warmth and simplicity of a bowl of soup bolsters and soothes as the rain clatters against the window and the mind whirls. Soup makes everything better.

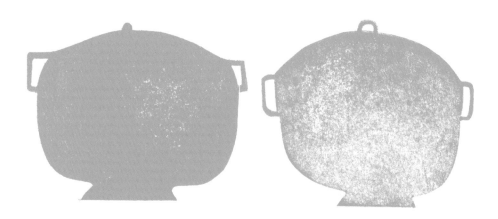

SOUP'S PLACE AT THE TABLE

Alhough it can certainly be a meal in itself, soup is often just the introduction, thanks to the switch from French to Russian service on fashionable tables in the 19th century. The impressive platters that covered the table, to be eaten all at once, and the large soup tureens placed at each end in the old *service à la française*, were cleared to make way for *service à la russe*, the style of dining we're familiar with today, in which dishes are served one at a time. Sitting down to a rapidly cooling feast meant that diners often took a few polite sips of soup before moving on to a heartier dish. Thus soup became a sort of appetiser, a habit that was cemented when the service style switched.

MULLIGATAWNY

Like kedgeree and curry, mulligatawny is part of the culinary legacy of the Raj, a cultural mishmash of traditional British soup and a spice-infused Madrassi broth or *rasam* known as *molo tunny,* or pepper water. The historian Lizzie Collingham suggests that, 'Mulligatawny soup was one of the earliest dishes to emerge from the new hybrid cuisine that the British developed in India, combining British concepts of how food should be presented (as soups or stews, etc) and Indian recipes.' The dish was invented to provide a familiar first course at dinner parties, but in her curry bible Madhur Jaffrey notes, 'A true mulligatawny soup is really a curry, a meal in itself. Anglo-Indian families often ate it for Sunday lunch, accompanied by rice, relishes and chutneys.' Having been adapted from a simple pepper water, it's the kind of recipe that invites experimentation. Add your own flourish or try Meera Sodha's version at the end of this chapter, made with parsnips, carrots and lentils.

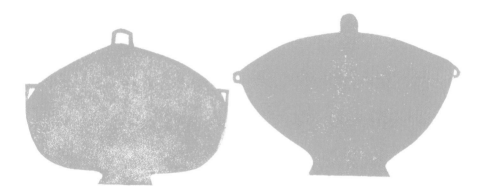

Noodle Soup for Perfection
by Livia Franchini

You string them up like pearls, ballerina
you're always thinking about pretty things
three bunches along the counter, a magic number
once, you rinse the onions before cutting
you rinse again so tears don't come up
your eyes/
              your eye makeup/unfurled
the leaves are senseless once they're scratched out

Third you cut the flesh up into circles
to set aside as toppings, rings/or
                           ringlets
your kitchen piled high with the reminders
fluorescent juice, the rind of onions staring
sprightly, very green where it rolls out of your bowl

A white and bright rectangle
the chopping board
the two pale twins of ginger and garlic
the small slant cut in your small finger
seals up with lemon yellow

You've brushed your hair ten times on each side
until it added to a hundred
an odd addition, to an odd bunch/
in winters like these what will a woman do, other
than pretend she is a woman who wears pigtails
tighten your fingers around a handful/think
about how cold you are even in summer
unpin the noodle, look up at your face from its reflection

      in the hot oil
              crack an egg.

Spice Tips
by Rachel Walker

KEEP IT FRESH

Old spices aren't dangerous, but they also aren't particularly useful as they lose potency over time. When buying spices it's best to stick to small amounts and replenish your supplies often. An annual clear-out is a good idea, to help keep track of what you have and avoid accidentally accruing ten different jars of cumin.

STORE SENSIBLY

Spices are happiest in an airtight container kept away from light or heat. Although a wall-mounted rack of glass jars may look pretty, spices are susceptible to sun-bleaching, so it's best to prioritise practicality over aesthetics to help keep them fresh for longer.

SEASON WITH FLAIR

Think beyond salt and pepper and look to your spice cabinet for inspiration. Whether drizzling spiced butter, tempering daal or simply sprinkling sumac, za'atar or *pul biber*, spices shouldn't be overlooked as a finishing touch.

BREAK THE RULES

Shichimi togarashi is a Japanese blend often served with noodles, but I love it sprinkled over grilled cheese on toast. I also keep a pinch pot of *pul biber* on our kitchen table – it can transform anything from fried eggs to grilled vegetables.

LAYER FLAVOURS

A strong set of the basic spices – turmeric, cumin, coriander – will get you far, but just a few inexpensive additions can make a big difference. Spices such as *amchur* (dried mango powder) and fenugreek are rarely used in isolation, but they build beautiful depth of flavour when used in collaboration with other spices.

DON'T SCRIMP

Spices are a relatively inexpensive part of a dish, but they're often the main source of flavour. Lax labelling means that you get what you pay for – for example, cheap 'cinnamon' could, in fact, be ground cassia bark – so it's worth spending a few pence extra and cooking with something really good.

A Menu for October
by Meera Sodha

PARSNIP AND CARROT MULLIGATAWNY SOUP

This hits the spot in a way many soups don't in that it will fill you up – but, if you're sceptical, you could eat it (as many people used to) with boiled rice spooned in for good measure.

Serves 4

3 tbsp rapeseed oil
1 large onion, diced
4 garlic cloves, crushed
3cm (1¼in) piece of fresh ginger, peeled and grated
1 green finger chilli, very finely chopped
250g (9oz) carrots, cut into 1cm (½in) cubes
250g (9oz) parsnips, cut into 1cm (½in) cubes
1 tsp ground cumin
1½ tsp ground coriander
150g (5½oz) dried red lentils, washed and drained
1.25 litres (2¼ pints) vegetable stock
Sea salt

Preheat the oven to 180°C/350°F/gas mark 4. Heat the oil in a deep-sided pan over a medium heat, then fry the onion for 5 minutes, stirring occasionally, until soft and translucent. Add the garlic, ginger and green chilli, stir-fry for a couple of minutes, then add the carrots and parsnips and cook for 6–8 minutes, stirring occasionally, until the onions are sticky.

Add a little water if the mixture is too dry, then add the cumin and coriander and stir for a minute. Add the drained lentils, stock and a quarter teaspoon of salt. Stir, bring the mixture to the boil, then turn down the heat to a whisper and simmer for 15 minutes, until the vegetables are tender. (If you're blending the soup, now is the time to blend it, adding more water if you prefer a thinner consistency.) Season to taste and serve.

PUMPKIN AND WALNUT BIRYANI

Because pumpkins are so often associated with Halloween or Cinderella's preferred mode of transport, it's easy to forget to actually eat them. In this recipe, the pumpkin is many things: a delicious ingredient in its own right, a host for spiced rice tangled with onions and nuts and, best of all, a very special dish to share at the table.

The type of pumpkin you buy is key here. Delica pumpkins are the best for flavour and sweetness, and their skin can be eaten, too, but a large Crown Prince or Kabocha squash would also work. Avoid the big orange ones, though – they're great for carving scary faces into, but not very nice for eating.

Serves 4–6

150g (5½oz) basmati rice
1.3–1.5kg (3lb–3lb 5oz) Delica pumpkin
1 tsp fennel seeds
1 tsp cumin seeds
¾ tsp ground cinnamon
4 tbsp rapeseed oil
1 large onion, finely sliced
4 fat garlic cloves, minced
1cm (½in) piece of fresh ginger, grated
1 tbsp tomato purée
1½ tsp Kashmiri chilli powder
275ml (9fl oz) hot vegetable stock
40g (1½oz) walnuts, chopped
100g (3½oz) cranberry sauce
Sea salt

Preheat the oven to 180°C/350°F/gas mark 4. Wash the rice under cold water, swirling it with your hand until the water runs clear, then drain, cover with cold water and leave to soak.

Cut the top off the pumpkin – keep the lid – and scoop out and discard the seeds (or keep to roast); if you've scooped out any flesh, dice and put it to one side. Sprinkle a little salt inside the pumpkin and rub it all over the exposed flesh. Crush the fennel and cumin seeds in a mortar until fairly well ground, then add the cinnamon.

Heat 3 tablespoons of the oil in a frying pan (skillet) over a medium heat, then add the bashed spices and onion and cook, stirring, for 12 minutes, until dark brown and starting to crisp. Set aside a tablespoon of the onion mix, then stir the garlic and ginger into the pan. Add the reserved diced pumpkin flesh, if any, along with the tomato purée and a teaspoon of the chilli powder. Cook for 3–4 minutes, until the mixture is dry, then add ¾ teaspoon salt, the well-drained rice and hot stock. Bring to the boil and cook, stirring regularly, for exactly 17 minutes, then take off the heat. Taste for salt, mix in the walnuts and spoon the lot into the pumpkin.

Put the reserved onions on top of the rice and cover with the pumpkin lid. Wrap the pumpkin tightly in foil like a badly wrapped present, place on a baking tray and bake for 70 minutes, or until a knife slips through the side very easily.

Mix the cranberry sauce with 1 tablespoon of oil and the remaining half teaspoon of chilli powder. Unwrap the pumpkin, place it on a fancy platter, cut it into wedges and serve with the cranberry sauce.

FENNEL SEED SHORTBREAD

Sometimes fennel seeds taste like fresh toast, sometimes like nuts and occasionally they taste aniseedy or a bit like liquorice – but all of these warm flavours marry perfectly together with rich, buttery shortbread. The inspiration for this recipe was my father. He is a big fan of eating fennel seeds after dinner in 'mukwas' as a breath freshener, and his favourite biscuit is shortbread.

Makes 12 biscuits

1½ tbsp fennel seeds
350g (10½oz) plain (all-purpose) flour
250g (9oz) cold unsalted butter
125g (4½oz) caster (superfine) sugar, plus extra for sprinkling

Preheat the oven to 160°C/325°F/gas mark 3.

Gently toast the fennel seeds in a dry frying pan (skillet) over a medium heat for 1–2 minutes, until you can smell them. Then crush them using a pestle and mortar and set to one side.

Put the flour into a bowl, add the butter, then use your fingers to rub the butter into the flour until it resembles breadcrumbs. Tip the ground fennel seeds in and mix through.

Next, add the sugar and knead the mixture into a ball. Wrap the ball in cling film and pop it in the fridge for 30 minutes to 1 hour.

When you take the dough out of the fridge it will be harder but you should still be able to work with it. Lay it on a sheet of baking paper and lay another sheet over the top. Using a rolling pin, slowly and evenly roll out the dough until it's around 2cm (¾in) thick. Transfer the dough to a baking tray and remove the top layer of baking paper.

Bake for 40 minutes, or until the shortbread is a pale gold colour. Once it is out of the oven, lightly sprinkle a handful of caster sugar over the top and cut into fingers. I find that 8cm x 3cm (3¼in x 1¼in) makes for a good-sized biscuit. Leave to cool before eating.

Reading List

Laurie Colwin, *Home Cooking*
One of the warmest, funniest food
books ever written, weaving together
memories, recipes and wild tales.

Jane McMorland-Hunter and Sue
Dunster, *Quinces*
The cultivation, history and cooking of
the most fragrant fruit of the orchard,
with useful sections on growing your
own tree.

Lindsey Bareham,
A Celebration of Soup
A global survey of the most
comforting of dishes in all its
variety, from the intensity of a clear
consommé to the hearty warmth of
a rich chowder.

Livia Franchini, *Shelf Life*
A whip-smart debut novel from this
chapter's soup poet, told through a
series of shopping lists.

Lizzie Collingham, *Curry*
The story of curry as it spread from the
courts of Delhi to the balti houses of
Birmingham, melding historical fact
with modern anecdotes.

Caz Hildebrand,
The Grammar of Spice
A stylishly illustrated A to Z that
touches on the historical, cultural,
culinary and medicinal aspects of spices.

Meera Sodha, *East*
Vegetarian and vegan recipes bursting
with colour from India, Thailand, Japan
and beyond.

November

THE COOK'S LARDER

Ingredients to look out for in November:

- Bergamot, cranberries, medlars
- Cardoon, cauliflower, cavolo nero, kohlrabi, parsnips, salsify
- Sea beet, sloes
- Mallard, partridge
- Raclette, Red Leicester, Reblochon

Morning mists linger in the damp November air, gauzy and ethereal, and the loamy smell of rotting leaves pervades the woods and country lanes. Prepare for the cold affront with sweetness: coat crisp, sharp apples in toffee, toast marshmallows until burnished and molten, fill a flask with mulled cider spiked with rum. Guy Fawkes Night calls for parkin, that sticky ginger cake from the north of England, eaten quickly and greedily around a bonfire.

Resist the urge to hibernate. Instead, wrap up well and head outside for bracing walks. It's not so cold yet that getting caught in a downpour doesn't have its comical side. The intensity of the weather can be all-consuming, hunched against the wind and rain, cocooned in umbrella solitude. Comfort is needed as you burst through the door, dripping wet, and food can be the greatest comfort.

Cooking even the simplest thing is an act of self-care. Gentle evenings in the kitchen call for dishes that demand time but not attention. 'Autumn cooking is not about instant flavours or assemblies of startling contrasts, it's about layering and waiting,' says Diana Henry. Cook pulses to a soothing softness, simmer robust stews with seasonal game, pile up mounds of buttery mashed potato and roast golden roots, their edges slowly browning.

And, of course, there must be pudding: treacle tart, apple crumble, steamed sponge puddings surrounded by moats of hot custard, pears baked with cinnamon and cloves in a rich red wine and every kind of pie — it is the month of Thanksgiving, after all, and there's nothing more universal than pie.

Medlars

UGLY DELICIOUS

The medlar is a strange fruit. It inspires both reverence and revulsion, largely due to its unusual ripening process. Once picked, it must be left to blet, a process of gentle decay that breaks down the starches into sugar. The firm, pale flesh gives way to a deep amber pulp, a 'delicious rottenness' as D.H. Lawrence describes it in his poem dedicated to the fruit: 'What a rare, powerful, reminiscent flavour / Comes out of your falling through the stages of decay.'

Like the quince and mulberry, the medlar is one of our forgotten fruits: once widely cherished, now more of a niche choice. A few centuries ago, the medlar was grown throughout Britain; before the arrival of sugar it was considered a popular wintertime treat. The bletted flesh is sweet and tastes of apple purée with undertones of citrus, date and apricot. The best medlars can be eaten as they are, but they're particularly good roasted with honey and eaten with cream, or baked into cakes and tarts. Take inspiration from Robert May's cinnamon-spiced recipe, published in 1660: 'Take medlars that are rotten, strain them, and set them on a chaffing dish of coals, season them with sugar, cinnamon and ginger, put some yolks of eggs to them, let it boil a little, and lay it in a cut tart; being baked scrape on sugar.'

Medlars are difficult to find in greengrocers, so look for jars of their jewel-coloured jelly to pair with game, roast meats, pâtés and cheese, or simply spread on toast.

BUTT OF THE JOKE

Due to its curious form, the medlar has often, quite literally, been the butt of jokes. Its ancient English name, 'openarse', tells you why. And in certain parts of France, it's still called *cul de chien* (dog's arse). It is the source of risqué references in Shakespeare's *Romeo and Juliet*, and a symbol of age and decay in Chaucer's prologue to *The Reeve's Tale*.

Let the Rot Set In
by Eli Goldstone

'*Tenderness and rot share a border*' Kay Ryan

Not all decay ruins: it can simply transform. I like cheeses that are washed with booze or brine to encourage bacteria to multiply on their rinds. The soft kind originates from the cellars of monasteries, the hard from the peaks of the Swiss Alps. Sluicing them this way makes them stink but stops them going bad. These sorts of cheeses taste best with dessert wine made from grapes that have been encouraged to rot on the vine. Sauternes, for instance. The best are produced by picking individual berries that have been infected by what is called 'noble rot'. The grapes are shrivelled and contain something like syrup.

My favourite conditions are the sort that encourage decay: warm and damp. More often than not there's something softening in my fruit bowl. Delicate, thin-skinned fruits rot first. A punnet of raspberries – the most tender fruit of all, pink and vulnerable as the underside of a cat's paw – often starts to mould on the shelf. An apple can sit determinedly in its rough jacket for a couple of weeks. You might cut away a bruise or a soft spot, throw it in a soup or a crumble where its texture counts for less, perk it up with spice or sugar. Thrown black into the freezer, ripe with nail varnish remover intensity, an old banana comes into its own in a no-nonsense cake made with wholewheat flour for breakfast, smeared with dulce de leche to stop it from being too worthy. Decay encourages invention, and I love it for that. Time dictates what we eat and when, even in a world where we can buy soft fruits in winter.

In Mexico, *huitlacoche*, also known as corn smut, or more enticingly as Mexican truffle, is served on tortillas at the back of enormous markets full of useful things, semi-precious stones and the tooth-numbing smell of chilli. The fungus is a blight turned into a delicacy. It tastes of corn and mushroom and also of dirt – deep-down dirt, ancient and transgressive, sweet and metallic. It has more nutritional value than the corn itself, being packed full of protein and lysine, an essential amino acid, and is perfect in an omelette. I'll never forget it. During the winter I spent living in Oaxaca, failing to write my second novel, my room was often peppered with fruit flies drunk on the heady perfume of a collapsing mango, brown thumbprints in its puckered yellow skin. This sort of fruit can be particularly good, almost fermented and jelly-like, perfect for covering in sharp grains of salt, lifted with a squeeze of lime.

Spiced Pumpkin Pie
by Nik Sharma

Of all the American holiday feasts, Thanksgiving is my favourite: it celebrates flavour and is a chance to gather together with family and friends. While the backbone of the dinner menu is familiar, there's plenty of opportunity to play with ingredients. Each year I try to paint the menu with aromas and tastes that I grew up with in India to help build a connection between my two worlds – and the character of this pumpkin pie does just that.

The pie is infused with warm and aromatic spices, a welcome treat as the temperature drops. A scoop of lightly sweetened, tangy crème fraîche is all you need to serve this with. You can use any type of pie crust you like; the recipe here is one I've used for years, given to me by a friend from grad school. It's made with hazelnuts, which add a wonderful nutty scent both to the pie and your kitchen as you bake. If you have a digital thermometer to hand, it will help to get the custard filling just right.

Makes one 23cm (9in) pie

For the pie crust:
57g (2oz) unsalted butter, cubed and warmed to room temperature, plus a little extra for greasing
57g (2oz) granulated sugar
1 large egg, lightly whisked
1 tsp hazelnut or almond extract
100g (3½oz) plain (all-purpose) flour
100g (3½oz) finely ground hazelnuts or almonds
¼ tsp fine sea salt

For the filling:
425g (15oz) unsweetened pumpkin purée
3 large eggs, plus 3 egg yolks
2 tsp ground ginger
1 tsp ground green cardamom seeds
½ tsp ground cinnamon
¼ tsp ground nutmeg
¼ tsp ground turmeric
4 tbsp honey
100g (3½oz) dark brown sugar
¼ tsp fine sea salt
125ml (4fl oz) full-fat milk
125ml (4fl oz) double (heavy) cream

```
1 tbsp cornflour (cornstarch)
2 tbsp water
```

```
Sweetened crème fraîche, to serve
```

Lightly grease a 23cm (9in) tart tin with a little butter.

To make the pie crust, place the butter and sugar in the bowl of a stand mixer and, using the paddle attachment, whisk on low speed for 5 minutes, until combined. Scrape the sides of the bowl down, increase the speed to medium and mix for a further 5 minutes, until light in colour.

In a small bowl, mix together the egg and nut extract. In a large mixing bowl, dry whisk the flour, ground nuts and salt.

Add the egg and nut extract to the butter-and-sugar mixture in the stand mixer and whisk on medium speed until combined, about 2 minutes. Add the dry ingredients and whisk again until combined, about 1 minute. Transfer the mixture to the prepared tart tin. Spread the dough out to cover the surface of the tin and the sides. Wrap the pie with cling film and refrigerate for at least 1 hour until firm, or freeze for up to 2 weeks in a resealable airtight bag.

To blind-bake the crust, preheat the oven to 180°C/350°F/gas mark 4 and set a rack on the lower level. Line a baking tray with baking paper. Place the tart crust on the baking tray. Prick the surface all over with a fork. Cover with a large sheet of baking paper and weigh it down with baking beans (or dried beans) to prevent the surface from rising during baking. Bake for 25–30 minutes until the sides just start to brown. Remove from the oven and allow to cool for 5 minutes. Remove the baking paper holding the beans.

To prepare the pie filling, place all the filling ingredients, except the cornflour and water, in a blender and blitz for a few seconds on high speed until the mixture is combined. You can also whisk the ingredients together in a large bowl. Transfer the mixture to a thick-bottomed saucepan over a medium-low heat. Mix the cornflour with the water to form a smooth slurry and whisk it into the pumpkin mixture. Whisk and stir for 10–12 minutes until the mixture thickens at 74°C/165°F (have your digital thermometer handy). Scrape the sides of the saucepan with a silicone spatula during cooking. Take off the heat. Set a sieve over a large measuring jug and strain the custard to remove any lumps.

Pour the custard into the pre-baked pie crust and bake for 25 minutes until the custard is set and a digital thermometer reads 85°C/185°F when inserted into the centre of the pie. The custard should be firm on the sides but slightly jiggly in the centre. Transfer to a wire rack and let the pie cool before serving with the crème fraîche.

The Life of a Thermos
by Tim Hayward

The Thermos sits at the back of the bottom shelf in my kitchen cupboard. You have to mine to find it, through strata of rarely used gadgets. It's a little rusty around the bottom rim, the plastic cup on the top is a probable mismatch and the tartan would be more associated with cheap, mass-produced shortbread than any actual clan. I found it in a smelly old fishing bag when I was cleaning out Dad's stuff and, obviously, I couldn't throw it away.

The Dewar or vacuum flask was invented by Sir James Dewar in 1892, a delicate double-walled vessel of silvered glass that, for a while, would slow the process of cooling or warming the liquid stored in it. The flask itself was usually clad in a protective layer of cork and then a decorated metal sheath: the 'Thermos' we know so well.

Both my grandfathers carried Thermos flasks through the war: one in the freezing fuselage of a bomber, the other to the factory where he built aero engines and at night to the anti-aircraft battery he manned, protecting his factory, town and family. During that era, men carried Thermoses in the bottom of a gas-mask bag, slung over a shoulder as they climbed cranes, dug holes, drove trains, manned lathes and won coal. By the time my father was going to work, there was an office kettle and he could stop at a transport caff when he was out on the road. But the Thermos would still come out, packed for long drives, family picnics and fishing trips.

I got the Thermos when I was sent to a horrible school, a miserable, repressive joysink, where my parents, bless their hearts, thought I might benefit from its brand of education. I have never been unhappier in my life, but Mum (who knew) understood that hot soup had therapeutic value. She could see that the essential element of the Thermos had never really been James Dewar's miraculous thermal engineering, but its magical ability to carry a piece of home, the hearth and the person – usually wife or mother – who had filled the thing before you left. Like a tribal fetish or saint's relic, it could hold spiritual power and transmit love.

I don't use the Thermos any more. I'll probably never pick it up and shake it to see if the fragile interior is still intact. I'll probably never taste again the stewed orange tea with evanescent undertones of coffee and the background redolence of Heinz Cream of Chicken. Maybe I don't need to carry 'home' in my bag; just a laptop is enough, and I can always grab a hot drink or soup wherever I am. It even feels a little embarrassing, oddly gendered – an accoutrement of masculinity that has outlived its role.

I still can't bring myself to dump it. Maybe I should dig out Dad's old rods and take it fishing, maybe I'll take it to the hill where the anti-aircraft battery stood, or maybe I'll keep it – it would make an admirable urn for my ashes.

WHAT TO KEEP IN YOUR THERMOS

Tea

This is what you'd expect to find in a Thermos. It needs to be brewed strong, preferably to the point of being orange and tannic. The tea is going to stew while it's being stored, so consider using UHT milk, which is slightly sweet and caramelised, or go full Singapore style and add condensed milk. So sweet it's an entirely different drink, but utterly gorgeous.

Coffee

Your barista is not going to be thrilled about filling your Thermos if you like milk-based coffees. Flat whites and cappuccinos depend so much on foam structure and can't survive storing.
If you can carry your milk separately, pour-over coffee can be held for ages in a Thermos, but my personal favourite is oily, Italian-style espresso. You lose the *crema* but it's rocket fuel.

Tomato soup

Straight out of the tin and poured in hot. This is what you take if you're sea fishing with Dad and you expect frostbitten fingers. Available on prescription in some regions.

Daal

The Thermos has a variety of medical uses but the best is carrying a really good daal to a friend's house when they're laid low by illness.

Martini

To sip a profoundly chilled Martini from a Thermos as you stand in a trout stream on a summer evening is one of life's exquisite pleasures.

A Menu for November
by Anna Del Conte

LEEKS IN A VINAIGRETTE SAUCE

This recipe has been in my repertoire for the last 30 years. As with quite a few of my best recipes, I owe it to my friend Myriam, an Italian and a very good cook, who is very generous with her recipes. The vinegary sauce works well with the sweetness of the leeks. If you haven't any stock to hand, make it with a bouillon cube. These leeks are good eaten at room temperature with plenty of crusty bread to mop up the juices.

```
Serves 4

8 medium-sized leeks
500ml (17fl oz) hot beef stock
4 tbsp extra virgin olive oil
2 tbsp balsamic vinegar
Juice of ½ lemon
1 tsp Dijon mustard
2 eggs
6 rashers back bacon, cut into small strips
1 tbsp small capers, rinsed
Sea salt and freshly ground black pepper
```

Heat the oven to 180°C/350°F/gas mark 4.

Trim the leeks, leaving some of the best green tops attached. Cut each in half lengthwise. Place them in an ovenproof dish in which they will fit in no more than two layers.

Pour the hot stock over the leeks and place the dish in the oven. Bake for 15–20 minutes or until tender when pierced with the point of a small knife. Lift the leeks out and place them on kitchen paper to dry. Keep the stock for a soup – it is very good.

To make the vinaigrette, put the oil, vinegar, lemon juice, mustard, salt and pepper in a bowl and mix well. Taste and adjust the seasoning, adding a little more lemon juice to your liking.

Boil the eggs for 4 minutes and peel.

Put a small frying pan on the heat, add the bacon and fry until it is crisp. Lift the bacon out of the pan with a slotted spoon and place it on kitchen paper to drain.

Spread one spoonful of the vinaigrette in a serving dish, lay the leeks on top (cut side-up) and then spoon the rest of the vinaigrette on top. Cut the eggs into small pieces and scatter over the top, together with the capers and bacon.

FETTUCCINE WITH SAUSAGE, MUSHROOM AND GREEN OLIVE SAUCE

In this dish, from the town of Ascoli Piceno in Italy's Marche region, the sauce is used to dress homemade fettuccine. The local olives, fat and meaty with their exciting and lively flavour, are a perfect foil to the sensuality of a rich pork sausage, while the whole dish is enlivened by the pleasing bitterness of the lemon zest. It is a superb sauce.

Serves 4

20g (¾oz) dried porcini
225g (8oz) coarse-grained pure pork sausages
1 tbsp olive oil
60g (2¼oz) unsalted butter
90g (3¼oz) brown mushrooms, thinly sliced
2 tbsp chopped flat-leaf parsley
1 tsp grated zest from an unwaxed lemon
1 garlic clove, very finely chopped
12–18 green olives, large and sweet, pitted and cut into strips
450g (1lb) fresh fettuccine or 300g (10½oz) dried egg fettuccine
2 tbsp extra virgin olive oil
Salt and freshly ground black pepper

Cover the porcini with boiling water and leave to soak for about an hour. Drain, rinse under cold water and dry them. Chop them coarsely and set aside.

Cut the sausage into thin rounds and put in a frying pan (skillet) with the oil over a medium heat. Fry for 10 minutes, stirring frequently.

Choose another frying pan large enough to hold the cooked pasta later. Heat the butter and add the mushrooms and the porcini. Sauté for 5 minutes over a lively heat. Season with salt and pepper and stir in the parsley, lemon zest and garlic. Cook for 1–2 minutes, then add the sausage. Turn down the heat and continue cooking for a further 5 minutes, stirring constantly. Add the olives and cook for 1 minute. Taste and check the seasoning.

Meanwhile, cook the fettuccine in plenty of salted boiling water. Drain, but do not overdrain, and reserve a cupful of the pasta water. Turn the pasta into the large frying pan and pour over the extra virgin olive oil and a couple of tablespoons of the reserved pasta water. Cook for 1 minute while tossing constantly and lifting the strands up high so that they are all glistening. Serve immediately, preferably from the pan.

PEARS BAKED IN RED WINE

The pears traditionally used in this recipe are Martin Sec, a fairly small, rust-coloured pear that grows in Valle d'Aosta. Williams or Rocha are good substitutes. Barolo, the wine in which the pears are poached, is one of the great wines from Piedmont made from Nebbiolo grapes. It is full-bodied and rich, ideal to counterbalance the sweetness of the fruit.

Serves 6

375ml (13fl oz) Barolo or other full-bodied red wine
Pared rind and juice of 1 unwaxed lemon
Pared rind and juice of ½ unwaxed orange
2 cloves
½ cinnamon stick
4 peppercorns
1 bay leaf
180g (6oz) caster (superfine) sugar
6 pears, ripe but firm

Heat the oven to 150°C/300°F/gas mark 2.

Put all the ingredients except the pears in a saucepan. Add 150ml (5fl oz) of water and bring slowly to the boil, stirring constantly to dissolve the sugar. Boil for about 15 minutes, stirring occasionally.

Wash the pears, leaving the skin and the stalk on. Choose an ovenproof dish into which the pears will fit snugly standing up. Pour the wine syrup around the pears in the dish and bake, uncovered, for 75–90 minutes, until the pears can easily be pierced by the point of a knife.

Stand a pear on each plate and spoon the syrup around it. They look very pretty. These pears can be served warm or cold, but not straight from the oven or chilled. If you like, you can hand around a bowl of whipped cream or crème fraîche.

Reading List

Christopher Stocks,
Forgotten Fruits
The fascinating and often rather bizarre stories behind Britain's rich heritage of fruit and vegetables – and a call to arms against homogeny.

Robert May,
The Accomplisht Cook
Perhaps the most important cookery book of the 17th century, written by England's first celebrity chef. It includes extravagant recipes such as a pastry stag filled with claret, and a tortoise stewed with nutmeg and sweet herbs, alongside simple instructions for porridge and sausages.

Eli Goldstone,
Strange Heart Beating
A darkly funny and seductive debut novel that explores the possessive undercurrents of love.

Nik Sharma, *Season*
Intriguing recipes that seamlessly blend influences from India, the American South and California, accompanied by beautiful photographs by the author. Try the apple masala chai cake.

Truman Capote,
The Thanksgiving Visitor
A short story inspired by the great American writer's Alabama childhood, featuring a Southern feast with stuffed turkeys, whipped sweet potatoes and a cold banana pudding.

Tim Hayward,
The Modern Kitchen
Every item in the kitchen has a story. Essays on the design, economics and social history of the heart of the home, and a portrait of our domestic lives.

Anna Del Conte,
Classic Food of Northern Italy
Definitive versions of classic dishes such as pesto, ragu and ossobuco from the doyenne of Italian cooking.

December

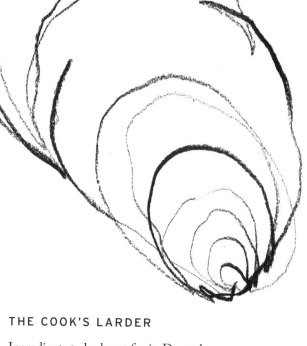

THE COOK'S LARDER

Ingredients to look out for in December:

- Clementines, dates, persimmons, pomegranates
- Brussels sprouts, celery, leeks, red cabbage, swede
- Wild onion
- Pheasant, turkey, woodcock
- Mont d'Or, Montgomery's Cheddar,
  Ossau-Iraty, Stilton

As the wind frightens the last leaves from the trees and hopes
for snow are dashed by wayward drizzle, the winter solstice
draws near. Frost creeps prettily along branches and windows,
doors stick in the stubborn cold and fine layers of ice crack
under heavy winter boots. Decidedly it's time to be indoors.

There is a sense of joyful anticipation at this time of year;
rolling celebrations and a chance to raise a glass to family
and friends. Mulled wine evokes a certain bonhomie, but
parties call for frivolous, sparkling things: add a fragrant
homemade bergamot syrup to a flute or coupe to conjure a
deceptively simple champagne cocktail. The French have a habit
of dipping sugary pink biscuits (*biscuits roses de Reims*) in
champagne, a sweet tradition worth taking up. 'A party where
there are enough nice things to eat has a warm, contented
sound, a sort of purr,' said Margaret Costa. 'Nothing gives
more of a fillip to a party that's beginning to flag than the
appearance of a tray of hot little things to eat, preferably
on sticks.' Never mind dinner, it's all about the snacks.

Then the happy chaos of Christmas morning arrives. Plumes of
steam billow from the kitchen, readying appetites for the
feast ahead. Of course, not everyone wants to overindulge at
Christmas. Elizabeth David, somewhat baffled by the traditions
and sentimentality of the festive season, insisted she would
prefer 'a smoked salmon sandwich with a glass of champagne
on a tray in bed'. Yet there is something undeniably magical
about a shared Christmas meal. It can weave a spell over those
gathered at the table, one that lingers long into the night.

The peaceful, gentle days after Christmas should be relished,
especially when there are leftovers to devour. Soon it will
be New Year's Eve — popped corks and generous toasts — and
time to begin all over again. What delicious things we have
in store.

Chestnuts

ROASTING ON AN OPEN FIRE

The sweet chestnut is sometimes called 'the grain that grows on trees'. It's almost as starchy as wheat, and can be ground into flour to make bread, pasta, cakes and *necci*, a type of Tuscan crêpe. Riffing on the carb theme, you can also use sweet chestnuts in a similar way to potatoes – they're excellent mashed and served with game such as pheasant and venison.

The Romans were cultivating sweet chestnut trees as early as 35 BCE, their armies marching on a diet of chestnut porridge. They ranked the nuts alongside the olive tree and the grapevine as plants important to civilisation, and so cultivated them in conquered lands. Yet history has not been kind to this once-lauded food. In many parts of Europe chestnuts have become associated with hardship, having seen communities through times of war and poverty. We often reject 'poor' food when prosperity returns, but flavour eventually lures us back.

Despite their name, sweet chestnuts are equally at home in savoury dishes. Their smoky sweetness works well in soups and stews as well as desserts, such as Castagnaccio (a type of chestnut cake) and Mont Blanc. Simply roasted, whether on an open fire or in the oven, they pair well with whisky and ale, or a piece of dark chocolate. Toss a handful of peeled chestnuts into a pan fizzing with butter, add salt and fresh oregano, and serve as a snack with a glass of red wine.

Chestnuts are good all winter (and you can buy them in jars or tins year-round), yet they always feel festive. Add them to stuffing or mix with sprouts for Christmas lunch. For dessert, take inspiration from the French and swap Christmas pudding with Bûche de Noël, a chocolate log filled with chestnut purée. Then finish your meal with one perfect marron glacé – poached in syrup, then glazed, they are incredibly sweet – served with tea or coffee.

Listen Good
by Kit de Waal

My father made enough Christmas cake to feed the whole of exiled Antigua. Every year we shrank from the endless instructions and preparations. Even on an ordinary day he'd shuffle between the sink and the stove, talking to himself while he made the dinner.

'Yes, a nice stewed chicken,' he would say. 'Skin the bird, chop some garlic and thyme. Not too much salt.'

We would try to drown him out with the radio or our bickering and complaints, but he would always carry on. 'Put them tight in the dish, like so, with pepper. Good.'

We used to think he liked the sound of his own voice and we'd mock his sing-song West Indian accent. 'Pass me de tometto sauce, no?' we would chime in his hearing, or 'I just want little, little rice with dis', or 'Mus come mek me a samwitch.' My sister had it down to a T, all his mannerisms and inflections.

Even before the baking started in the first week of December, we began to dread the deliveries. When the cakes were cold, he would double wrap them in greaseproof paper, then aluminum foil, and pack them in a cardboard box, a dozen or more. He would load them, and us, into the back of his Austin Minor and skid us through the winter streets to drop them off one by one. On the salted front doorsteps of narrow terraced houses, we stamped and shivered, one eye on the daggers of ice that dangled from the roof.

'Come in, come in! Come! Yes, come!'

It was a long day of visits to seldom-used front rooms and steamy kitchens, of repeated stories about back home, when the sun shone and you felt it in your bones, of pinched cheeks and 'Look, how they've grown', endless comparisons, endless measurements.

'Bless you, Arthur,' the old women said. An old man with snowy hair and rheumy eyes balanced on his walking sticks and shook my father's hand.

That summer, as every summer, he prepared the fruit for soaking as usual.

'Run down to Fraser's,' he said, and the three of us took a shopping bag and dragged home packets of dried fruit, blue-black raisins, golden sultanas, leathery prunes – pounds of the stuff.

He scalded five enormous Kilner jars and stood them steaming and dangerous on the draining board. He brought out bottles and bottles of sherry and brandy, rum the hue of his skin and small corked bottles of a nameless liqueur that smelt sickly sweet and reminded me of my father's barber. Then he sharpened the kitchen knife on the back step, scraping it at an angle against the concrete, back and forth until the blade shone along its curved edge. He stoned prunes with a swift curl of his wrist, chopped them into fine pieces against his palm.

We groaned when he gave us jobs, accompanied as always by his running commentary.

'Line up the jars, line them up. Listen good. Now, take a bag of fruit each. Kim you is raisins, Tracey you is sultanas, Dean you is prunes. Take a handful, drop them in turn by turn, mix them up, go round each other, that's it, fill the jars, good, bit by bit, that's it, right to the top.'

We feigned incompetence, messing up his system, making him reorganise us and explain again what he was trying to do. 'You have to make sure you don't have too much of anything. Look here, too many raisins. Dean go easy on the prunes, not so much, not so much.'

We giggled, spilt our cargo and squashed it underfoot.

'Listen good,' he said, wiping the floor. 'When the cake is done, you want it just right, each one must have a little bit of everything, all the same.'

'Yes, Dad,' we said flicking raisins behind his back.

My father was slow that year, distracted. As he filled the jars with pints of spirits, it dribbled down the side and pooled at the base. We dipped our fingers in, wincing and coughing as it burned our tongues. He screwed the lids tight and stowed them in the far recesses of the pantry, underneath the stairs where the fruit would plump and swell in the dark while Halloween and Guy Fawkes Night came and went and the trees were stripped bare.

After the second stroke left him mute and twisted, we sat with my father in the sitting room while the nurse told my mother how to massage his arms and legs. At the front door she reminded her to wash and shave him, keep him warm, feed and talk to him, move him from room to room and keep his mind alert. After she had gone my mother went upstairs to cry.

No dinner was made that night, nor the one after that. We scavenged the cupboards and took money from my mother's purse. We fed our father sandwiches and biscuits and took soup to my mother, who sat by his side as bowed and silent as he was.

When the cupboards were bare, we went to the pantry and found, right at the back, the fruits he had put to soak. We carried them out, heavier somehow, the bulging sultanas pressed up tight against the glass. My mother said that the fruit would keep, that next year maybe when our father was better, he would be able to wield his special mashing spoon against pounds and pounds of sugar and butter in the special Christmas bowl; that he might, when he could speak again,

tell us how many nutmegs to grate, how much ginger syrup to drip, how many cinnamon barks to grind beneath the pestle, how deep the purple-black tracks of vanilla essence through the thick batter, and eggs? How many? And when? And what shelf in the oven and how hot? He might make his cakes again. He might.

In the end, she gave us the money and we ran to Kent's and back. We made the kitchen ready and my mother brought him in. He shuffled to an easy chair, and we helped to arrange his arms and legs, a pillow for his neck so he could watch us. Under his eye, we broke the job into child-size pieces and chanted the instructions we had heard but never listened to.

'Make it smooth, now. Can you taste the sugar? Beat it again.'

'One more egg, just one, don't let it curdle. Use the flour.'

'Sift it good, you don't want no lumps.'

Last of all, we folded in the fruit from the Kilner jars, spooning in the liquid until the mixture matched our memories.

'Is this it, Dad?'

His mouth moved but we got no answer.

We greased tin after tin until the small hours, long after my father was put to bed, and in the morning the sideboard was lined with our offerings – square, round, loaf tins and shallow Pyrex dishes used in desperation.

We could smell the alcohol days after the cake was done, long after we shook hands with my father's elders and brought home their herbal tonics, ancient potions and prayers for his recovery.

The smell of rum and brandy, burnt sugar and spice clung to the curtains and cushions all the way through Christmas and into the New Year when my father crumbed the first sticky slice with his one good hand. His eyes closed slowly and he smiled.

'Just right,' he said. 'Just right. You listen good.'

The Scent of Advent

by Anja Dunk

A house that smells of pine and spice is something of a wonder. It is the scent of Advent, the run-up to Christmas, and it is both my favourite smell and time of year. Despite December being dark and cold, or perhaps because of it, we gain so much light and warmth through cooking and eating.

At home we don't have a cosy fireplace to sit around. I long for one, I won't lie, especially when Christmas cards with this very image start arriving in the post. Instead, we take comfort in our oven, which is constantly aglow with baking – a little beacon of light and warmth in the corner of the room, which crackles and puffs at you just the same, emitting wafts of cinnamon, cardamom, ginger, anise and clove. You could almost argue that an oven is actually a better antidote to the cold.

The pitch-black mornings of December trick you into feeling as if you're stealing hours from the night, making the day seem longer, not shorter. Breakfast by candlelight and Advent sunrises (around 8am) rival any summer sunset, with precious light returning in a warm blaze of orange and red. Hob breakfasts of rib-sticking clove and apple porridge or treacly, cinnamon-stewed prunes engulf the kitchen in a cloud of steam, which somehow heightens the resinous scents of the tree. This contrasting smell of cold climates mixing with tropical ones, through the use of spice in cooking, has become synonymous with Christmas. It's a smell you can't fake, and nor should you ever want to – no scented candle or room fragrance could ever replace it.

For me, the best way to achieve a heady hit of Advent is by baking spiced biscuits to hang on the tree.

SPICED TREE BISCUITS

These are a cross between a British and a German classic, the ginger nut and the lebkuchen. They have the texture and crunch of the former and the spicy notes and honey flavour of the latter.

I like to use a tree-shaped biscuit cutter, but any festive shape works well. The biscuits are very crunchy, so good with a cuppa, but they do soften over time. They keep well for 2–3 weeks, no need for airtight storage. We eat them straight off the tree; any stale ones make a perfect base for a New Year's trifle.

```
Makes about 50 cookies
(depending on the shape and size of the cutter)

250g (9oz) rye flour
250g (9oz) plain (all-purpose) flour
2 tsp ground cinnamon
2 tsp ground ginger
1 tsp ground cloves
½ tsp ground cardamom
½ tsp ground anise
½ tsp fine sea salt
150g (5½oz) unsalted butter
225g (8oz) light brown sugar
9 tbsp runny honey
2 tsp bicarbonate of soda (baking soda)
2 tbsp just-boiled water
```

Preheat the oven to 200°C/400°F/gas mark 6. Line two baking trays with baking paper.

Mix together the flours, spices and salt in a large bowl. Melt the butter, sugar and honey in a saucepan over a medium heat, stirring constantly until the mixture is an even consistency. Pour the honey mixture into the dry ingredients. Dissolve the bicarbonate of soda in the just-boiled water and pour this on top of all the other ingredients. Beat everything together with a wooden spoon until a stiff dough forms.

Place the dough on the work surface – there's no need to flour or oil as this dough is magically non-stick. Roll the dough out until it's 3mm (⅛in) thick. Cut out shapes with your biscuit cutter and place them on to the lined trays, leaving 1cm (½in) between each biscuit for spreading. Now you need to make the hole for the ribbon to go through. Using a chopstick, press a hole into the biscuit near the top and move the chopstick in a circular motion so that the hole is about 5mm (¼in) in diameter.

Bake in the oven for 8 minutes until golden brown. When you take the biscuits out of the oven, the hole will have closed up but you should still be able to see where it was. Using the chopstick, repeat the hole-making process. Leave the biscuits on the tray for a further minute to stiffen up a little before moving on to a wire rack to cool.

Thread loops of candy cane-striped string through the holes in the biscuits and hang them on the tree. If you go the extra mile and ice the biscuits they do look incredibly pretty.

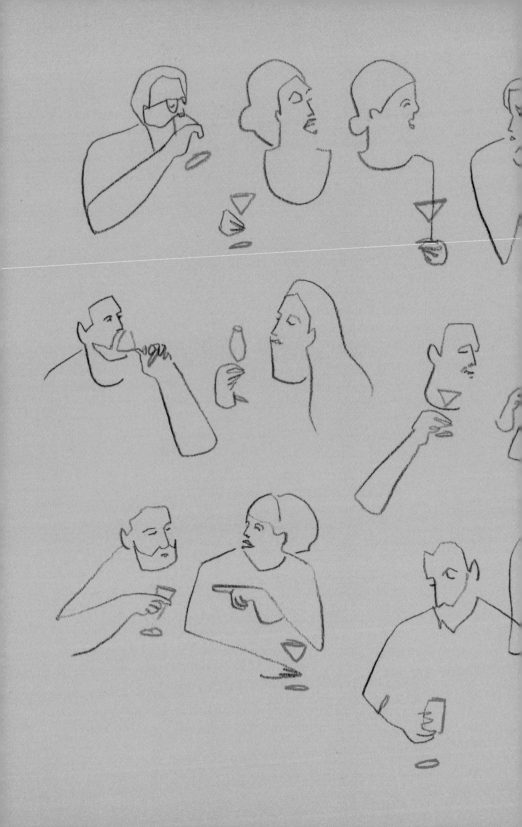

A Festive Cocktail

by Kay Plunkett-Hogge

Faced with the question, 'What's the best cocktail for…?', I have only one answer. The Martini. As clear and bright as a high note from B.B. King's guitar. So much the Platonic ideal of drinking perfection, they probably served them at The Symposium. Surprisingly, this answer sometimes disappoints, especially in December when people want something that looks festive. Never mind that the Martini is as deep and crisp and even as anything King Wenceslas could hope for.

At this point, I could steer people towards the Negroni, but given that rejecters of the Martini are most likely gin refuseniks, that isn't going to work. Instead, I give you the Boulevardier: equal parts bourbon, Campari and sweet vermouth, on ice, with an orange slice. Were it created in these unimaginative times, it would most likely be called a Bourbon Negroni, given that the Negroni was almost certainly its inspiration.

The Boulevardier first appears in print in Harry MacElhone's *Barflies and Cocktails*, published in 1927. MacElhone credits its invention to Erskine Gwynne, editor of the Parisian English-language monthly *The Boulevardier*. The writer Paul Clarke describes it as the Negroni's autumnal cousin. I would argue it's more wintry. No foliage ever turned this red. This drink is redder than Santa's coat. The bourbon provides its warming frame, the bitters and vermouth the devil and the angel on its shoulders.

And what should we eat with this winter's ambrosia? Not mince pies, that's for sure. No withered fruit, black with decay, in a pastry coffin. No. Instead, let's serve up macaroni cheese studded with bits of crispy bacon.

Not so long ago, I had a long chat with Desmond Payne, the master distiller of Beefeater and all-round gin god, about the merits of eating macaroni cheese with a Negroni. Given bourbon's fondness for bacon – if you've never tried an Old Fashioned made with baconised bourbon, you're missing out – the Boulevardier makes a perfect pairing for a gloomy winter's day: the cheesy pasta nourishes the core of one's being; the bourbon tickles the cockles of the heart; while the Campari and vermouth offer Italianate hope of warmer months to come.

Choosing the Cheeseboard

by Hero Hirsh

The most traditional approach to the Christmas cheeseboard is based on selecting a range of styles; the classic hard, soft and blue combination is tried and tested, and Cheddar, Brie and Stilton are a cheese shop's bestsellers at this time of year. Most will add in a goat's or sheep's milk cheese and a washed rind to tick all the boxes. I tend to serve cheeses as a trio. In part this is because there is an expectation that a cheesemonger will bring a selection, but also because I get overexcited and find it hard to choose any fewer. I do feel, though, that a single cheese served with perfect accompaniments is a much more confident choice. The less there is on the plate, the greater the emphasis on quality, and it's an opportunity to showcase one incredible cheese. Whatever you choose, it should be crowd-pleasing and in perfect condition, so be sure to taste it before purchasing.

OSSAU-IRATY

Ossau-Iraty is a six-month-aged sheep's milk cheese from the Pyrenees. It should have a fudgy consistency and a sweet, nutty, almost caramelised flavour with the kind of strong herbal notes you might expect from the summer mountain pastures where the sheep graze. It marries well with nuts and dried fruit and stands up to bold red wines.

Perfect pairing: St Emilion, crisp charcoal crackers and prune confit.

STILTON

Stilton has a long association with festive tables as autumn rains create a second growth of grass, leading to rich milk being produced 3–4 months ahead of Christmas. This creamy milk is the key to delicious Stilton; the cheesemakers will work to ensure that all the cream content remains in the cheese, leading to a buttery, melt-in-the-mouth consistency. A good Stilton will have a yellowish paste, even blueing and, when ripened fully, it will be free of crumbly or white patches. Stilton is available in miniature or jarred form, but the absolute best is cut from a full-size truckle.

Perfect pairing: Sauternes or vintage port, oatcakes and slivers of perfectly ripe pear.

MONT D'OR

Mont d'Or or Vacherin du Haut-Doubs is only produced between August and March, and tends to arrive in cheese shops at the start of October. The earliest cheeses of the season can be a little restrained in flavour with a squidgy texture. It's worth waiting a month or two for oozing pastes and full pine-resin notes coming from the spruce bark in which the cheese is wrapped. Try baking Mont d'Or in its box as you might a Camembert: make a little cross shape in the top rind to poke in some thyme and garlic slices and a splash of white wine; after 20 minutes in the oven you will have a wonderful bubbling fondue for dipping crusty bread. It is equally good (and liquid) at room temperature; cut the top rind off and serve it with a spoon.

Perfect pairing: Vin jaune or a Blanc de Blancs champagne, crusty bread and a spoon.

Don't Mess with the Trimmings

by Ed Smith

Christmas lunch is a fundamentally flawed meal of too many moving parts. So now 'tis the season to review your repertoire and not be tempted by the glittery allure of the flashy and the new. It's comforting seasonal nostalgia we crave at this time of year, after all.

Despite the yuletide deluge of recipes in newspapers and magazines, the reality is that most dishes are set in stone: roast potatoes, obviously; stuffing – preferably two, one pork-based, one bread-based; chipolatas wrapped in bacon; cranberry sauce; bread sauce; gravy; parsnips. Just cook them as you always have.

The exceptions to my miserly approach are carrots and sprouts – two sides that are ripe for experimentation and easily benefit from quick embellishment: fresh herbs, compound butters, nuts, lardons, spice mixes, glazes and so on.

In the context of a Christmas meal, with its many roasted elements, sprouts and carrots sit best where the cooking medium involves water. Both should be pulled from their heat source just prior to the point where 'undercooked' becomes 'just right'; they'll reach, but not go past, their peak as you wait for family and friends to come to the table. And those blanched/boiled/steamed/braised vegetables add brightness and colour to otherwise beige plates. A handful of embellishment guidelines follow:

SPROUTS

Essential: butter and lots of black pepper
Other seasonings: celery salt; ground cloves; ground cardamom; anchovy butter; balsamic vinegar; pomegranate or cherry molasses; citrus zest
Potential partners: lardons; pancetta; lardo; cooked chestnuts; clementine segments; dried cranberries; pomegranate seeds

CARROTS

Essential: butter and flaky sea salt
Other seasonings: browned butter; extra virgin olive oil; parsley (as fine as dust); chopped chervil; fresh thyme leaves; citrus zest; carrot juice; orange juice; star anise; nutmeg; ginger powder; dill seeds; maple syrup; honey; sherry vinegar and Dijon mustard dressing
Potential partners: toasted hazelnuts; sesame seeds; pecans; roast onions or shallots

A Menu for December

by James Ramsden

CHRISTMAS LEFTOVERS SANDWICH

If you were ever to eat Christmas lunch with me and my siblings, you might well find yourself wondering where our appetites had gone. True, we don't hold back on crisps and olives and other titbits that might be kicking about while we open presents and get politely tipsy. But later you might notice us declining seconds of roast potatoes, shunning Christmas pudding, forgoing chocolates and candy canes. Not only this, but there's an unmistakable, if below-the-radar, sense of resentment towards those – other halves, distant relatives, the dog – who are helping themselves to yet more turkey.

Perhaps the gig is up and you've guessed what we're up to. As any discerning food-loving fool knows, the best thing about Christmas lunch is not Christmas lunch. No, it's the sequel: Christmas Lunch 2: This Time it's Leftovers. This undeniable truth partially explains our forbearance, but it doesn't entirely explain the way we dodge the Christmas pudding and chocolate. The problem is that somehow, at some point, we got into the habit of having our (first) Christmas leftovers sandwich on Christmas Day itself. This was largely down to our grandparents' insistence that we ate at 1pm, so by the evening we had the gastric bandwidth to take on a version of what follows below. We just couldn't wait any longer.

How these sandwiches are assembled does of course depend on what you've had for your Christmas lunch. As a starting point, strip the turkey, or goose, or capon, or whatever you've enjoyed 4–6 hours before (saving the bones for stock). Assemble the vegetables and as many condiments as you can reasonably dig out, and set to work with this as your guide.

Meat
A combination of meats is something to aim for. Of course, part of the point of this operation is to use what you have, but there's nothing wrong with shopping for some extras with this sandwich in mind – bacon for crisping, ham hock for oomph, quality chorizo for spice, mortadella for that deli meat angle. You want about 150–170g (5½–6oz) in total, shredded into bite-sized bits and gently warmed in a little stock or gravy.

Condiments

We make a 'bread sauce mayo', although it doesn't contain any actual bread. You'll need to get hold of some fresh yeast and roast it in a hot oven until toasty and crisp. Let it cool and whizz it up. Fold this, along with ground clove and onion powder, through mayonnaise to taste. Otherwise, consider Hellmann's (or better, Kewpie) a blank canvas for vigorous zhuzhing: think garlic, sriracha, mustard, Maggi and Chilli Crisp (that jar of crunchy, spicy deliciousness with the angry-looking woman on the front, available in Asian supermarkets). All of these are excellent, if not eaten together. Anything containing MSG wins bonus points. The amount of mayo needed slightly hinges on the type of bread you're using, but 2–3 tablespoons should be about right. And if ever there was a time for double-condiment action, this is it. Cranberry sauce, if that's your bag. Some sort of chutney. Quince paste. Harissa. Go nuts.

Vegetables

A large fistful of watercress, possibly some gem lettuce for neutrality. Something pickled – preferably red cabbage, carrots or onions. Not gherkins, though. Delicious as they are, they're too sweet and assertive here. I used them one Christmas and regretted it – while stubbornly eating the lot. Cornichons, on the other hand, particularly if you've gone down the turkey-plus-ham route, are very much recommended. Stuff in a good bunch of herbs: try parsley (lots), coriander (some), mint (sparingly). Sprouts are optional, although I prefer these as a sort of canapé while making the sandwich. Don't let parsnips anywhere near it.

Bread

White bloomer all the way, thickly sliced. Toasting optional. Aficionados of *Friends* will remember the 'moist maker' in Ross's Thanksgiving leftovers sandwich, a thin layer of gravy-soaked bread that sits in the middle. I'm all for it.

Wild cards

If you're making this late on Christmas Day, it's possible you've put away a few drinks and are feeling creative. Not forgetting the more-isn't-always-more caveat, keep in mind:

- Crisps in any sandwich are encouraged.
- I'd personally swerve cheese, but it's worth considering something that's not overly assertive – say, Gruyère or Parmesan.
- Is there anything that isn't improved by anchovies? Now's the time to find out.
- Add pickled jalapeños for spice and zing.

Reading List

Ria Loohuizen, *On Chestnuts*
Recipes for everything from chestnut pancakes to marrons glacés, with hints on sourcing, grinding your own flour and roasting chestnuts on an open fire.

Kit de Waal,
My Name is Leon
A moving novel about love, identity, fraternal bonds and home, set in 1980s Britain.

Anja Dunk,
Strudel, Noodles & Dumplings
A celebration of modern German home cooking, proving that there is more to German food than bratwurst and Black Forest gâteau.

Kay Plunkett-Hogge,
Make Mine a Martini
Cocktails and canapés for fabulous parties – and, most importantly, how to make a flawless Martini.

Michael Paterniti, *The Telling Room*
Set in rural Castile, a rambling tale of love, betrayal, revenge and the world's greatest piece of cheese.

Ed Smith, *On the Side*
Side dishes take centre stage. A clever cookbook complete with a recipe directory to help you find the perfect accompaniment, whatever you are cooking.

James Ramsden, *Do-Ahead Christmas*
Full of practical advice for making festive food in advance, so you're not left frazzled on the big day. Start with a tangerine whisky sour.

Charles Dickens, *A Christmas Carol*
A classic Christmas story full of spirits and ghosts, wickedness and redemption, but also roast goose, apple sauce, chestnuts and a Christmas pudding 'like a speckled cannon-ball'.

Author Index

Acknowledgements

First published in the United Kingdom in 2020 by

Pavilion
43 Great Ormond Street
London
WC1N 3HZ

Copyright © Pavilion Books Company Ltd 2020

Text copyright © Miranda York 2020*

Illustration copyright © Louise Sheeran

ISBN 978-1-91164-160-5

A CIP catalogue record for this book is available from the British Library.
10 9 8 7 6 5 4 3 2 1

Reproduction by Mission
Printed and bound by Toppan Leefung Printing Ltd. China
www.pavilionbooks.com

Publisher: Helen Lewis
Design: Atwork
Illustration: Louise Sheeran
Project editor: Sophie Allen
Copy editor: James Hadley
Production manager: Phil Brown

*except for all text acknowledged on pages 174-175

Thank You

To Stephanie Milner for sparking the idea, and my editor Sophie Allen for giving me so much freedom with my first book and patiently answering approximately one million questions. To Katie Cowan, Helen Lewis, Isabelle Holton, Komal Patel and everyone at Pavilion who has helped bring The Food Almanac to life.

To all the contributors: this book would not be what it is without your words, wisdom and beautiful stories.

To Will Perrens for your patience and obsession with fonts. To Louise Sheeran for making anything look fabulous with just a few strokes. And James Hadley for your discerning eye. I wouldn't trust anyone else with my words.

To Diana Henry for your guidance, and for writing the most wonderful books, which are always by my side. To Celia Sack at Omnivore Books in San Francisco for straight talking, and kick-ass book recommendations. And to my friends: Liz for kindly reading some of the first drafts; Lindsay and Sarah for helping with final checks; and Juliet, Aimee, Anna, Linda, Toral, Beth and Almaz for cheering me on.

To the great food writers of the past who have inspired me and made me a better writer, in particular Laurie Colwin, M.F.K. Fisher and Jane Grigson. I cherish my well-thumbed, second-hand copies picked up at book stalls and charity shops.

To everyone who has supported my company At The Table over the years – bought the magazine, attended events, listened to the podcast, watched films and generally indulged my obsession with food and words.

To Ross, for your love. To my parents, for everything.

ABOUT THE AUTHOR

Miranda York began her career as a food, travel and culture journalist, writing for publications such as the *Financial Times*, *Vogue*, *How To Spend It* and *Harper's Bazaar* before founding At The Table, a creative platform that explores and celebrates food culture. She has since curated over 100 events, published an independent food magazine, recorded a podcast series, produced short films and launched an artisan food market in Bermondsey, London. Miranda was named one of Code's 100 Most Influential Women in Food and has been shortlisted for both the Jane Grigson Trust Award and the Fortnum & Mason Food & Drink Awards. A born-and-bred Londoner, her favourite restaurants are to be found under old railway arches and along the narrow streets of Soho. She also has a serious weakness for brioche. *The Food Almanac* is her first book.

atthetable.co.uk